GLOBAL CHANGER

STUDENT'S BOOK AND WORKBOOK

STARTER

MAURICIO SHIROMA, VERONICA TEODOROV,
LIZ WALTER AND KATE WOODFORD WITH PAULO MACHADO

CAMBRIDGE
UNIVERSITY PRESS

CONTENTS

* This material can be downloaded from the Digital Resource Pack.

WELCOME!

HELLO

1 0.01 **Read, listen, and repeat.**

Jayla: Hi, I'm **Jayla**. Nice to meet you. What's your name?

Anthony: Hi! My name's **Anthony**. Nice to meet you, too.

LOOK!

My name **is** … / My name**'s** …

What **is** / What**'s** your name?

2 **Change the words in blue. Then practice the dialogue with a partner.**

CLASSROOM OBJECTS

3 0.02 **Look and number the words 1–6. Then listen, check, and repeat.**

eraser 4
pen ______
pencil ______
book ______
dictionary ______
notebook ______

THE ALPHABET

1 0.03 **Listen and repeat.**

A B C D E F G H
I J K L M N O
P Q R S T U V
W X Y Z

2 **Color the vowels: A in blue, E in brown, I in black, O in red, U in white. Color the consonants green.**

3 0.04 **Listen and write the words.**

1 green
2
3
4
5
6

USE IT!

4 **Complete the chart for you.**

	Me	My Partner
a name		
a school object		
a color		

5 **Work in pairs. Partner A: Spell your words. Partner B: Write the words for your partner. Take turns being A and B.**

LOOK!

a | pen
| book

an | eraser

NUMBERS 1–20

1 0.05 **Listen and repeat.**

0	1	2	3	4	5	6	7	8	9	10	11	12
zero	one	two	three	four	five	six	seven	eight	nine	ten	eleven	twelve

13	14	15	16	17	18	19	20
thirteen	fourteen	fifteen	sixteen	seventeen	eighteen	nineteen	twenty

2 **Work with a partner. Count by twos.**

Two!

Four!

Six!

3 0.06 **Listen and repeat. Then practice with a partner.**

How old are you?

I'm 12. How old are you?

I'm 11.

DAYS OF THE WEEK

4 0.07 **Listen and repeat.**

Monday Tuesday

Wednesday Thursday

Friday Saturday Sunday

5 0.08 **Listen and write the days of the week.**

1 Friday

2 ______

3 ______

4 ______

5 ______

MONTHS OF THE YEAR

6 0.09 **Listen and repeat.**

JANUARY · February

March · April · May

June · July · AUGUST

September · October

November · December

7 **Practice with a partner.**

Partner A: Say a number between 1 and 12.

Partner B: Say the corresponding month of the year and spell it.

Six!

June! J-U-N-E

NUMBERS 20–100

1 0.10 **Listen and repeat.**

20	21	22	23	24	25	26	27	28	29
twenty	twenty-one	twenty-two	twenty-three	twenty-four	twenty-five	twenty-six	twenty-seven	twenty-eight	twenty-nine

30	40	50	60	70	80	90	100
thirty	forty	fifty	sixty	seventy	eighty	ninety	one hundred

2 0.11 **Listen and circle.**

1	3	13	30	5
2	5	15	50	4
3	32	52	62	14
4	9	19	99	40

3 **What's the date today? Write the day, the month, and the number.**

Today is ....

TELLING THE TIME

4 **Match the clocks with the times below.**

- eleven o'clock
- five fifteen
- ~~four fifteen~~
- nine o'clock
- twelve forty-five
- two thirty

1 four fifteen

2 ....

3 ....

4 ....

5 ....

6 ....

LOOK!

What time is it? / What's the time?

1 0.12 **Look at the clocks and answer the questions. Then listen and check.**

1 What time is it in New York City?

It's seven thirty.

2 What time is it in Tokyo?

It's ______________________.

3 What time is it in London?

It's ______________________.

4 What time is it in LA?

It's ______________________.

CLASSROOM LANGUAGE

2 0.13 **Match the classroom language (1–6) with the pictures (A–F). Then listen and check.**

1 How do you spell *pencil*?
2 Look at that book.
3 What does *book* mean?
4 Write in this notebook.
5 Read this text.
6 Listen to that music.

A

B

C

D

E

F

LOOK!

This book.

That book.

1 WHO Am I?

UNIT GOALS

- Talk about your favorite things.
- Read a digital poster.
- Listen to a dialogue.
- Learn about students around the world.
- Talk about your personal information.

THINK!

1 Look at the image and write words in English.

2 Why are you special?

VIDEO 1.1

1 Say three things in the video that are important to us.

2 What sports are in the video?

VOCABULARY IN CONTEXT

1 Check (✓) the things that are true for you.

FAVORITE THINGS

A MY FAVORITE THING:

○ cell phone

○ bike

B MY FAVORITE PLACE:

○ home

○ school

C MY FAVORITE ACTIVITY:

○ music

○ sports

D MY FAVORITE CLOTHES:

○ jeans

○ school uniform

2 1.01 **Look at the images and complete the phrases. Then listen, check, and repeat.**

1 
A green cell phone

2 
A white ....

3 
My blue and white ....

4 
A black ....

5 
My awesome ....

6 
Popular ....

7 
My blue ....

8 
My favorite ....

3 **Write words from Exercise 2 in the circles.**

PLACES

CLOTHES

THINGS

ACTIVITIES

USE IT!

4 **Complete the sentences so they are true for you. Use a dictionary to help you. Then tell your partner.**

1 My favorite thing is ....

2 My favorite place is ....

3 My favorite activity is ....

WORKBOOK p.113 PRACTICE EXTRA

READING

1 **Look at the poster. Check (✓) all the elements that you see.**

- ◯ date and time
- ◯ long texts
- ◯ images
- ◯ title

2 1.02 **Read and listen to the poster. What is it about? Check (✓) the correct option.**

- ◯ important events at Meridian Forest School
- ◯ favorite things for 6th grade students
- ◯ the special students and teachers at Meridian Forest School

3 **Read the poster again and complete the sentences.**

1. Students __________ in 6th grade are **awesome**.
2. The t__________ are **cool**.
3. The m__________ is **great**.
4. The d__________ is **happy**.

THINK!

What is special about your class? In the poster, write a sentence about you, a friend, a thing, or your class. Use the bold words in Exercise 3.

WORKBOOK p.115

LANGUAGE IN CONTEXT

1 **Look at the examples below and complete the sentences from the poster.**

Verb *to be* Affirmative (+)	
Long Form	**Short Form**
I **am** Olivia.	I'm Olivia.
You **are** my friend.	You**'re** my friend.
He/She **is** two, and he/she **is** very happy!	He**'s**/She'........ two, and he**'s**/she**'s** very happy!
It **is** cool!	It'........ cool!
We **are** awesome!	We'........ awesome!
They **are** cool!	They**'re** cool!

2 **Change the underlined parts of the sentences. Use the example to help you.**

1 The teachers are great! They're great!
2 Flamenco is a type of music and dance. ....
3 My friend and I are happy. ....
4 Evelyn is my favorite friend. ....
5 Arthur is a cool student. ....

3 **Circle the correct words.**

1 Sarah *is* / *are* my teacher.
2 Max *am* / *is* my dog.
3 My jeans *is* / *are* blue.
4 My bike *is* / *are* at home.
5 I *'m* / *'re* a student.
6 We *is* / *'re* friends!

LOOK!
Max is my dog.
He's my dog.

4 **Complete the text with the correct forms of the verb *to be*.**

My name's Maria and I [1] 'm 12 years old. I [2] .... in 6th grade at Meridian Forest School. My favorite thing [3] .... my cell phone. My favorite friends [4] .... Lucia and Marco. They [5] .... cool!

USE IT!

5 **Complete the text so it is true for you. Then tell your partner.**

My name [1] .... and I [2] .... years [3] ....
I [4] .... in [5] .... grade at [6] .... School.
My favorite thing [7] .... my [8] .... My favorite friends are [9] .... and [10] .... They [11] .... !

LISTENING AND VOCABULARY

1 Look at the image. Audrey is ...

◯ in the classroom. ◯ at the yoga club.

2 1.03 Listen to the dialogue and check your answer.

3 1.04 Listen to the first part of the dialogue again and check (✓) the correct answers.

1 The dialogue is about ...
◯ registration at a new club.
◯ registration at a new school.

2 Yoga classes are ...
◯ on Friday. ◯ on Wednesday.

4 1.03 Listen to the dialogue again and complete the information about Audrey.

MERIDIAN FOREST SCHOOL

YOGA CLUB REGISTRATION FORM

Activity: ....
First Name: Audrey ....
Last Name: ....
Age: .... Grade: ....
Address: .... Liger Street ....
Home Phone Number: 555- ....

5 1.05 Match 1–7 with a–g. Then listen, check, and repeat.

1	Jones	a	grade
2	15 Park Road	b	name of school
3	13	c	phone number
4	Green Tree School	d	address
5	7th	e	first name
6	555-5281	f	age
7	James	g	last name

WORKBOOK p.112 and p.113

LANGUAGE IN CONTEXT

1 **Complete the questions from the dialogue with the words below.**

• ~~What~~ • How • Who • How old

Wh- questions		
***Wh-* Questions**	**Answers**	**Me**
What 's your phone number?	It's 555-5436.	
________ is your teacher?	Mr. Avery.	
________ are you today?	I'm good, thanks.	
________ are you?	I'm 12 years old.	

2 **Write answers to the questions in the chart that are true for you.**

3 **Complete the chart. Use the correct forms of the verb *to be*.**

Verb *to be* Negative (-)	
Long Form	**Short Form**
I **am not** Olivia.	I'**m not** Olivia.
You **are not** my favorite friend.	You'**re not** my favorite friend.
He/She **is not** very happy!	He'**s**/She'**s** not very happy.
It ________ **not** cool!	It'**s not** cool!
We **are not** awesome!	________ **not** awesome!
They **are not** cool!	________ cool!

4 **Correct the sentences so they are true for you. Use the example to help you.**

1 I'm in 8th grade. I'm not in 8th grade. I'm in 6th grade.
2 I'm nine years old. ________
3 My teacher is Ms. Gonzalez ________
4 My phone number is 555-5550. ________
5 My friends are Flora and Oliver. ________

USE IT!

5 **Ask your partner questions with the words below and complete the chart with his/her answers.**

Name	Last Name	Address	Teacher	Age	Phone Number

WORKBOOK p.112 and p.114 PRACTICE EXTRA

AROUND THE WORLD

www.globalteenstudents.net

HOME | WHO WE ARE | BLOG | JOIN

Sunday, May 21
(updated every day)

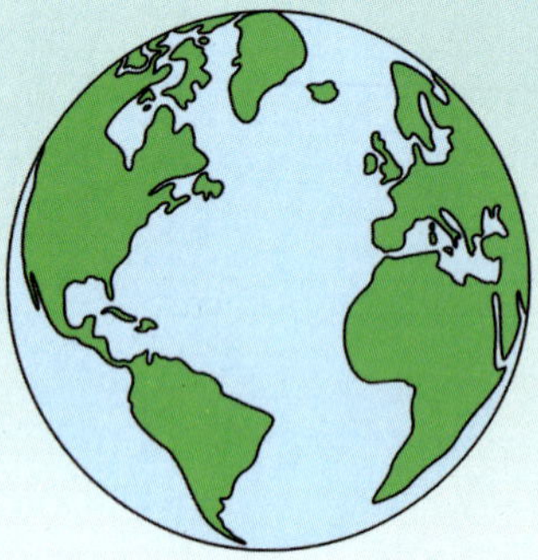

GLOBAL TEEN STUDENTS

By Students for Students,
We Are the World.
Let's Make Friends!

Students from different cultures around the world are on our web page. Let's meet three of them today!

LUKA, CROATIA

Hi, I'm Luka. I'm 13 years old and I'm a student. This is my camera, and this is my identity: my beautiful country and my photos of it.

Comments:

POST

CAMILA, HONDURAS

Hey, I'm Camila, and I'm 12. For me, family is very important. When I'm with my family, life is fun! My friends are important too, but my family is first.

Comments:

POST

KABALI, NAMIBIA

Hello! My name's Kabali. I'm 11 and I like music. But music is not my favorite thing. Nature is! Nature is very important to me and my community.

Comments:

POST

1 **Look at the web page. Complete the website address.**

www...

2 1.06 **Read and listen to the web page and check (✓) the correct answers.**

1 **What's it about?**
- ◯ world problems
- ◯ students of the world

2 **Who's on the web page?**
- ◯ students
- ◯ students and teachers

3 **How old is Kabali?**
- ◯ 11
- ◯ 12

3 **Read the web page again. Check (✓) what's important for the students.**

	Luka	Camila	Kabali
nature	◯	◯	◯
family and friends	◯	◯	◯
photography	◯	◯	◯

WORDS IN CONTEXT

4 **Find the words on the web page and then write them in your language. Use a bilingual dictionary to help you.**

1 beautiful
....

2 country
....

3 photo
....

4 fun
....

THINK!

Find three photos of your country that are important for you. Why are they important?

WEBQUEST

Learn more! Check (✓) *True* or *False*. Croatia, Honduras, and Namibia are on the same continent.

◯ **True** ◯ **False**

VIDEO

1.2

1 What is Kasia's favorite activity?

2 What is Trevor's favorite activity?

SPEAKING

GIVING PERSONAL INFORMATION

1 **Look at the image. The dialogue is about ...**

○ dance. ○ music.

2 1.07 **Read and listen to Ellis and Audrey.**

Ellis: Hi, I'm **Ellis**. What's your name?
Audrey: I'm **Audrey**.
Ellis: How old are you?
Audrey: I'm **12**.
Ellis: Me too.
Audrey: You're great!
Ellis: Oh, really? Thanks! **Ballet** is my favorite **activity**.
Audrey: Yes, it's **cool**.
Ellis: Let's text! What's your phone number?
Audrey: It's **555-5436**.
Ellis: Thanks!

LIVING ENGLISH

3 **Complete the mini dialogues with the expressions below.**

• You're great! • Me too. • Let's text.

1 A How old are you?
B I'm 11.
A ....

2 A What's your phone number?
B It's 555-9867.
A OK, ...

3 A Ballet is my favorite activity.
B ....
A Oh, really? Thanks!

4 1.08 **Listen and repeat the expressions.**

PRONUNCIATION /uː/

5 1.09 **Listen and repeat.**

Me **too**!

Yes, it's **cool**.

6 1.07 **Listen to the dialogue again. Then practice with a partner.**

7 **Role play a new dialogue. Follow the steps.**

1 Change the words in **blue** to write a new dialogue in your notebook.
2 Practice your dialogue with a partner.
3 Present your dialogue to the class.

YOUR DIGITAL PORTFOLIO

Record your dialogue. Then upload it to your class digital portfolio.

PRACTICE EXTRA

2 ENGLISH EVERYWHERE!

UNIT GOALS

- Talk about countries, nationalities, and languages.
- Read a forum.
- Listen to a radio show.
- Learn about English around the world.
- Write a post on an online forum.

THINK!

1 Where is English around you?
2 Why is it important to learn English?

VIDEO 2.1

1 Say two reasons why people need English to communicate.
2 Which countries do you see in the video?

VOCABULARY IN CONTEXT

1 2.01 **Look at the web page and complete the nationalities with the words below. Then listen, check, and repeat.**

- ~~American~~
- Brazilian
- British
- French
- Japanese
- Mexican
- Russian
- South African
- Spanish

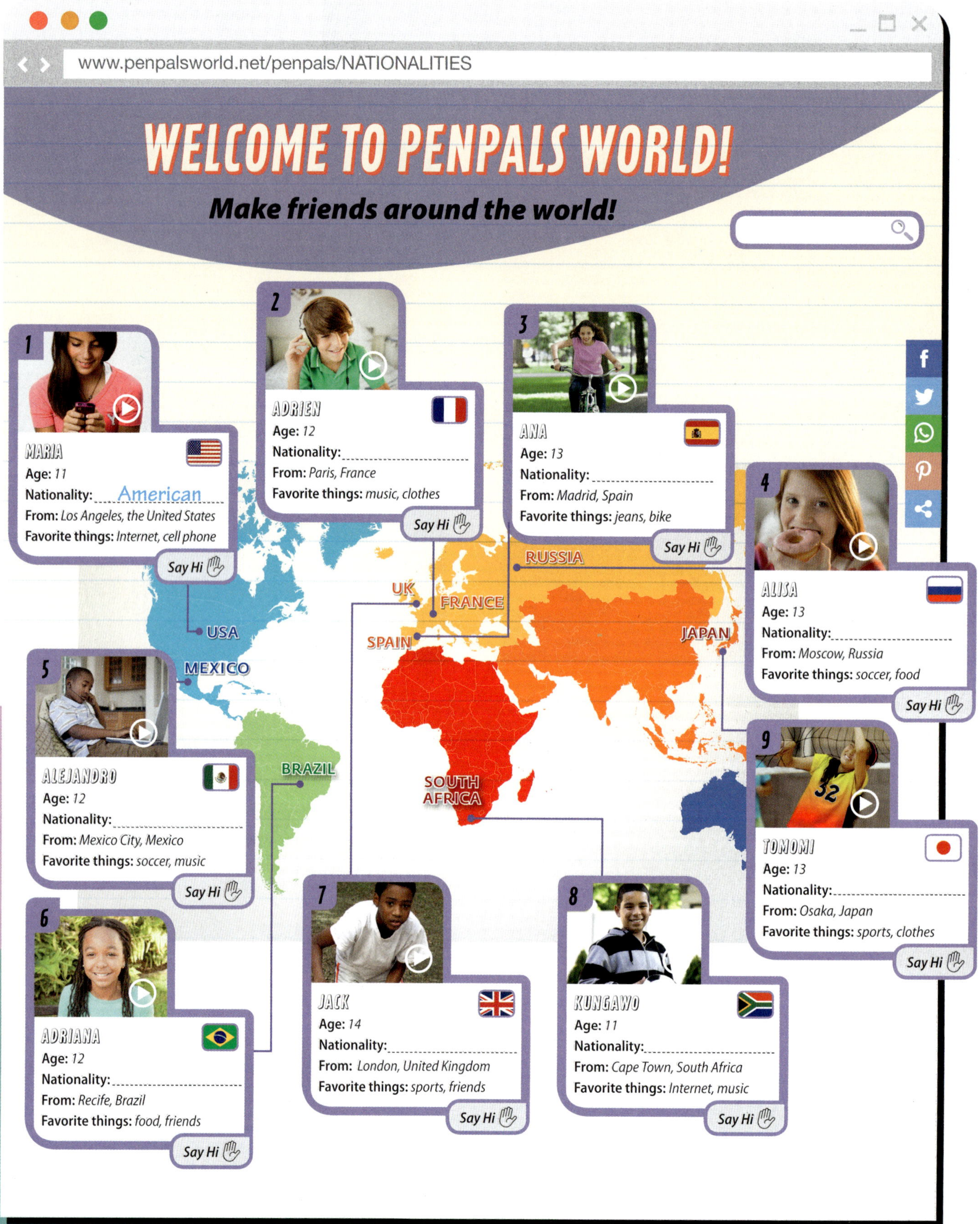

2 2.02 **Complete the chart with the countries or nationalities. Use the web page to help you. Then listen, check, and repeat.**

	Flag	Country	Nationality
1		Brazil	Brazilian
2		The United States	____r__c__n
3		South Africa	South ________n
4		___a__________	Japanese
5		R__________a	__________n
6		Spain	S__________h
7		______________	M__________
8		The United Kingdom	B__________h
9		F__________	__________

LOOK!

Use **CAPITAL LETTERS** with countries and nationalities.
I'm from the **U**nited **S**tates.
I'm **A**merican.
I'm from **M**exico. I'm **M**exican.

3 **Look at the web page again. Where are they from? Complete the sentences.**

1 Adrien is from France. He's French.
2 Ana is from __________. She's __________.
3 Kungawo is from __________. He's __________.
4 Tomomi is from __________. She's __________.
5 Jack is from __________. He's __________.
6 Alisa is from __________. She's __________.

USE IT!

4 **Work in pairs. Partner A: Say the name of a country. Partner B: Say the nationality. Take turns being A and B.**

WORKBOOK p.117 PRACTICE EXTRA

READING

www.penpalsworld.net

Forums >> General >> People

Masonboy10

Posted at 10:32

Hey guys! How about a game? Post TWO images and people guess your nationality or your country. These are my two pictures. What is my nationality?

REPLY

UnicornsAreAwesome

Posted at 10:35

Masonboy10. Are you from the United Kingdom? Hmm. Oh, no! You're from the United States. You're American! What about me? Where am I from? English is the official language in my country.

REPLY

McCupcake

Posted at 10:42

Beautiful! Is it the Maracanã Stadium? Are you from Rio de Janeiro? Wait, no, you're not. English is not the official language of Brazil!! 🙂 Are you South African? Oh, yes, you are. That's the Cape Town Stadium! Now guess MY nationality.

REPLY

Monte@home

Posted at 11:15

Wait! Is it Mexico? Oh, yes, it is! 🙂
I'm Mexican, too!
Look! Where's Mariana, my pen pal, from?

REPLY

UnicornsAreAwesome

Posted at 11:18

That's Copacabana beach. Is she from Brazil?

REPLY

Monte@home

Posted at 11:22

Yes, she is! 🙂
Good job!

REPLY

1 **Look at the text, images, and design. What is it? Check (✓) the correct answer.**

◯ a magazine article ◯ a forum

2 **What is the objective of this type of text? Check (✓) the correct answer.**

◯ to express an opinion

◯ to talk to different people

3 2.03 **Read and listen to the text. Write *T* (true) or *F* (false) next to the statements.**

1 Masonboy10 is from the United Kingdom. F
2 UnicornsAreAwesome is from South Africa. ....
3 McCupcake is from Brazil. ....
4 Two people are Mexican. ....
5 Monte@home is from Spain. ....

THINK!
What two pictures represent your nationality? Why?

WORKBOOK p.119

LANGUAGE IN CONTEXT

1 **Look at the examples below. Complete the sentences from the forum.**

Verb *to be*		
***Yes/No* questions**	**Short Answers**	
Am I right?	Yes, **I am**.	No, **I'm not**.
Are you from Rio de Janeiro?	........., you are.	No, you ....
Is he/she/it from South Africa?	........., **he/she/it is**.	........., **he's/she's/it's not**.
Are we Mexican?	........., **we are**.	........., **we're not**.
Are they from Brazil?	........., **they are**.	........., **they're not**.

Where ... from?			
I	**Where am I from?**	**I'm from** the United Kingdom.	**I'm not from** the United Kingdom.
you	**Where are you from?**	**You're from** Brazil.	**You're not** from Brazil.
they	**Where are they from?**	**They're from** Mexico.	**They're not** from Mexico.
he/she/it	**Where's he/she/it from?**	**He's/She's/It's from** Japan.	**He's/She's/It's not from** Japan.

2 **Write questions. Use the words in parentheses.**

1 
(you / Russia?)
Are you from Russia?
No, I'm not. I'm from South Africa.

2 
(your teacher / the United Kingdom?)
....
....

3 
(your cell phone / Japan)
....
....

4 
(your classmates / Brazil)
....
....

5 
(your friend / France)
....
....

LOOK!
Are you from Rio? Yes, I'm from Rio.
Yes, **I am**.
Is he a student? Yes, he's a student.
Yes, **he is**.

USE IT!

3 **Your partner is a famous person. Interview him/her.**

What's your name?
My name's ....
Are you Spanish?
No, I'm not. I'm ...

WORKBOOK p.116 and p.118 PRACTICE EXTRA

LISTENING AND VOCABULARY

1 2.04 **Look at the pictures. What are their names in English? Listen, check, and repeat.**

1 
ketchup

2 
....

3 
....

4 
....

5 
....

6 
....

7 
....

8 
....

2 2.05 **Listen to the radio show. Number the words in the order you hear them from 1–8.**

..... chocolate	..... hamburger	..... hotel	..... jeans
..... ketchup	1 pizza	..... restaurant	..... taxi

3 **What is the radio show about? Check (✓) the correct answer.**

○ English in Brazil ○ favorite words

4 2.05 **Listen to the radio show again. Write *T* (true) or *F* (false) next to the statements.**

1 Caio and Gabriela are on a radio show. T
2 Caio is from Brazil. .....
3 *Jeans* is a Spanish word. .....
4 There are English words and expressions in Brazilian Portuguese. .....
5 The word *chocolate* exists in many different languages. .....

USE IT!

5 **What are your favorite English words? Make a list. Then compare with a partner.**

....

WORKBOOK p.116 and p.117

LANGUAGE IN CONTEXT

1 Circle the correct answer according to the information in the radio show.

Possessive ('s)
Caio and Gabriela**'s** topic is English *in Brazil / on the radio*. Caio**'s** first language is *English / Portuguese*. Children**'s** favorite word is *chocolate / pizza*.

2 Complete the phrases.

John

1 

John's
notebook

Josh and Clara

2 

....
dog

Lisa

3 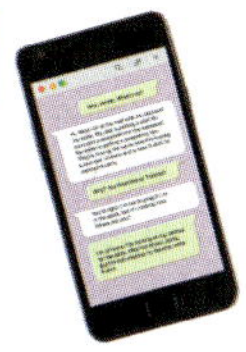

....
cell phone

The people

4 

....
favorite band

3 Complete the sentences in the chart with the words below.

• Its • His • Their

Personal Pronouns	Possessive Adjectives	
I'm **Brazilian**.	**My**	first language is Portuguese.
You're a good student.	**Your**	English is good.
He's a radio show host.	....	name is Caio.
She's from Japan.	**Her**	nationality is Japanese.
It's a pizza restaurant.	....	name is *Dino's Pizza*.
We're soccer fans.	**Our**	favorite team is *Barça*.
They're American.	....	country is the United States.

LOOK!
Use *their* for boys and girls.
Sergio and Katia's bikes.
Their bikes.

4 Circle the correct possessive adjectives.

1 Gabriela is on the radio. I like *her / my* radio show.
2 This is my friend. *His / Its* name is Marco.
3 We're from Mexico. *Her / Our* nationality is Mexican.
4 This is my school. *Our / Its* name is Park School.
5 This is Jane's bike and this is Max's bike. *Their / His* bikes are blue.

USE IT!

5 Complete the questions and answer them for you. Then interview your partner.

Questions		Me	My Partner
What's	name?	....	....
What's	favorite color?	....	....
Who's	friend?	....	....
What's	phone number?	....	....

6 Write four sentences about your partner.

WORKBOOK p.116 and p.118 PRACTICE EXTRA

ACROSS THE CURRICULUM

GEOGRAPHY

English is Everywhere!

Are you an English student? Good for you! Look at these facts about the English language:

1/5

English is a global language. About 1.5 billion people in the world are English speakers. That's 20% of the world population!

380 million

But only 380 million people in the world are "native" English speakers. They're from countries where English is the first language or native language: Australia, the United Kingdom, the United States, and others.

English is the language of science, commerce, sports, and tourism!

Are you a tourist? Are you on a plane? English is the official language for pilots. Your pilot is an English speaker!

English words are in different languages in many countries. In Brazil, many English words are very popular!

80%

Technology, computers, and social media are places for English, too! Over 80% of the words on computers are in English.

English words are common in Japan, too!

スーパー (suu-paa): supermarket
ホテル (ho-te-ru) hotel
レストラン (re-su-to-ran): restaurant

So, be part of this community! Speak English and communicate with the world!

1 **Look at the infographic. Circle the correct words to make a true sentence.**

This infographic is a *visual* / *long* text with *opinions* / *facts*.

2 **What's the infographic's central idea? Check (✓) the correct answer.**

- ◯ English as an official language
- ◯ the number of English speakers in the world
- ◯ the importance of English around the world
- ◯ English words in Japanese

3 **Scan the infographic and match the numbers (1–4) with the facts (a–d).**

1 7.5	a number of English native speakers in the world
2 380,000,000	b number of English speakers in the world
3 4/5	c world population, in billions
4 1,500,000,000	d proportion of English words on computers in the world

4 2.06 **Read and listen to the infographic. Complete the information.**

1 Two countries where English words are common, but people don't speak English as a first language:

Brazil and Japan .

2 Three countries where English is the native language:

__________, __________, and __________.

3 English is important in these activities:

__________, __________, and __________.

4 English is the official language for this profession:

__________.

WORDS IN CONTEXT

5 **Complete the sentences with the expressions below.**

• ~~native speakers~~ • social media • global language • native language • official language

1 Brazilian English students are not native speakers of English.
2 English is the __________ of the FIFA World Cup.
3 English is a __________. People speak it all over the world.
4 *Facebook*, *Twitter,* and *Instagram* are all examples of __________
5 Portuguese is the __________ of Brazilians.

WEBQUEST

Learn more! Where in the world is English the official language?

THINK!

Why is English important to you?

VIDEO

2.2

1 How many singers in the video sing in English?
2 Say the countries you hear in the video.

WRITING

1 2.07 **Read and listen to the post from a forum. What's the topic? Check (✓) the correct answer.**

◯ an online game ◯ a popular movie ◯ English words

www.penpalsworld.net

Forums >> General >> Languages | English Words Every Day

LavenderLiz

Posted at 4 p.m.

Hello, everyone!
I'm Brazilian, from Porto Alegre. Portuguese is our official language in Brazil, but English words are very popular. They're everywhere: restaurant names, foods, places, computers, etc. Here's my list: **download**, **Wi-Fi**, **playlist**, **videogame**, and **notebook**. My favorite word is playlist, because music is fun! How about you? Where are you from? What are your everyday English words? What's your favorite? Write a comment about it.

COMMENT SHARE LIKE

2 **Read the post again. Who is the post for? Circle the correct answer.**

People in *the forum* / *Italy* / *your country*.

3 **Read the post again and answer the questions.**

1 Which phrase is a greeting?
   Hello, everyone!
2 Find words for nationality, origin, and language.
3 Which phrase introduces a list of English words?
4 Find four questions for the reader.

LOOK!
How about you?
= And you?

4 **Write a reply to the post.**

1 Take notes: Write the name of your country, your city and your language. Make a list of common everyday English words for you. Then underline your favorite word.
2 Write your comment. Use the elements in *1*.

5 **Switch your comment with a partner and check his/her work. Use the checklist below.**

◯ Name of the country?
◯ List of English words?
◯ Favorite word?

YOUR DIGITAL PORTFOLIO

Review your text and write the final version. Upload it to the class portfolio for everyone to see!

REVIEW
UNITS 1 AND 2

VOCABULARY

1 Circle the odd one out.

1 sports / music / pizza
2 chocolate / hamburger / clothes
3 school uniform / taxi / jeans
4 school / bike / cell phone

2 Complete the interview with information about you.

1 What's your last name?
....
2 How old are you?
....
3 What's your address?
....
4 What's your phone number?
....

3 Put the letters in the correct order to complete the sentences. Where are the people from?

1 She's from IECXMO ....MEXICO.... .

2 She's from PNAJA ....

3 He's from CFNAER ....

4 She's from APNIS ....

4 Complete the sentences with the correct nationality.

1 I'm from Brazil. I'm ....Brazilian.... .
2 She's from Russia. She's ....
3 We're from the United Kingdom. We're ....
4 He's from South Africa. He's ....

5 Match the questions (1–5) with the answers (a–e).

1 Are you happy?
2 Is he cool?
3 Who are they?
4 How old are you?
5 Is she your teacher?

a No, he's not.
b They're my friends.
c I'm 12.
d No, she's not.
e No, I'm not.

6 Read the text. Then write and answer the questions.

Hi, I'm Alicia Patel, and I'm 12. I'm from Spain. I'm a student at the International School, and I'm in grade 7.
Joshua and Nina are my friends. We're in the same class. Joshua is from the United Kingdom, and Nina is from the United States. We're international students.

1 Alicia / Spain? Is Alicia from Spain? Yes, she is.
2 Alicia / teacher? ....
3 Alicia / sixth grade? ....
4 Joshua / the United Kingdom? ....

LANGUAGE IN CONTEXT

7 Look at the pictures and write sentences.

1 Isabella / bike / blue

Isabella's bike is blue.

3 Isaac / cell phone / black

2 Hugo / English / dictionary / new

4 Felipe and Kathy / favorite / food / pizza

8 Complete the sentences with the words below.

- ~~her~~
- his
- my
- our

1 Anna is my friend. *Her* last name is Green.

2 We're French. ______ country is France.

3 He's a student. ______ name is Frank.

4 I am Brazilian. Brazil is ______ country.

CHECK YOUR PROGRESS

I CAN...

- **talk about favorite things.**
- **use the verb to be to give personal information.**
- **talk about countries and nationalities.**
- **use possessive adjectives and 's.**

LEARN TO LEARN

Dictionary Entry

entry/word — bike

grammar function — *noun* [informal]

pronunciation — UK /baɪk/ US /baɪk/

meaning — **short form of "bicycle":**

translation — *bicicleta*

Source: https://dictionary.cambridge.org/dictionary/english-portuguese/bike

3 WHERE'S HOME?

UNIT GOALS

- Talk about different parts of a house and furniture.
- Read about a house.
- Listen to a video chat.
- Learn about houses around the world.
- Talk about your house and furniture.

THINK!

1 Imagine you live in this house. What are your favorite things about it?

2 Why is home important?

VIDEO 3.1

1 Say what types of homes are in these places: towns and cities, the countryside, on water.

2 What three things does the video say are important in a home?

VOCABULARY IN CONTEXT

1 3.01 **Complete Katia's messages with the words below. Then listen, check, and repeat.**

• bathroom • ~~bedroom~~ • dining room • kitchen • living room • yard

Places at Home

1 This is my ______ bedroom ______.
It's small, but nice.

2 Here's the ______________.
It's really modern!

3 The ______________ is
awesome. It's very big!

4 This is the ______________.
It's really nice!

5 Here's the ______________ –
and Julia's cat!

6 Look at the ______________ – and
the bikes. They're very old!

LOOK!

really + adjective
It's **really** nice!
very + adjective
It's **very** old.

2 3.02 **Where are the things? Write the places with the words in Exercise 1. Then listen, check, and repeat.**

1 In the bedroom.
2 In the ______.
3 In the ______.
4 In the ______.
5 In the ______.
6 In the ______.

1 
2 
3 
4 
5 
6 

3 3.03 **Look at the images and circle the correct words. Then listen, check, and repeat.**

A *small* / *big* house

A *small* / *modern* apartment

A(n) *old* / *modern* kitchen

A(n) *old* / *nice* bathroom

A *nice* / *big* bedroom

4 **Complete the chart with words from Exercises 2 and 3.**

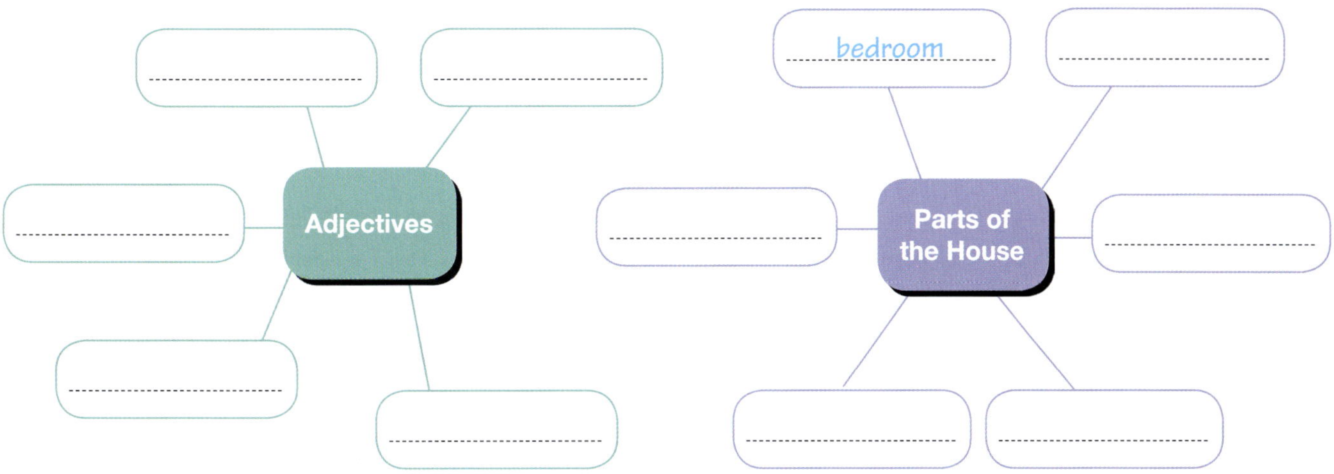

USE IT!

5 **Write sentences about your house. Use the words in Exercise 4. Then tell your partner. Are your houses similar?**

1 My bedroom is small.
2 My ______ is ______.
3 My ______ is ______.
4 My ______ is ______.

READING

1 **Look at the text and the image, and answer the questions. Check (✓) the correct answers.**

1 **What type of text is this?**
◯ a blog ◯ a dialogue from a chat app

2 **What is the topic of the conversation?**
◯ a trip ◯ a house

Hi, I'm Jakob. I'm from Norway. I'm 11.
This is my home. It's different! It's a stilt house.
There's one bathroom, and it's small! There are three small bedrooms. My favorite place is my bedroom. It's not big, but it's awesome. There's a bed, and a table (and my cell phone)! There isn't a yard, but there's a place for my bike. My bike is my favorite thing!
My family's favorite place is the living room. It's big and modern. There's a kitchen and a dining room in one room. It's small and old, but very nice. My friend, Filip, is in the dining room. Today, there aren't any hamburgers, but there is pizza. Yummy!
Where are you from? Is your home different?

2 3.04 **Read and listen to the text. Complete the chart about Jakob's home with the correct number of rooms.**

Jakob's Home	
kitchen/dining room	1
bathroom	....
yard	....
living room	....
bedroom	....

3 **Read the text again and answer the questions.**

1 Where is Jakob from?
Jakob is from Norway.

2 How old is he?
....

3 What is Jakob's favorite place?
....

4 What is Jakob's favorite thing?
....

5 What is his family's favorite place?
....

6 Who is Filip?
....

THINK!
What's your favorite place in your house? Why?

WORKBOOK p.123

LANGUAGE IN CONTEXT

1 **Look at the examples below and complete the sentences from Jakob's blog.**

There is/There are	
Affirmative (+)	**Negative (-)**
There's a kitchen.	**There** .... a yard.
There .... three small bedrooms.	**There** .... **any** hamburgers.

LOOK!

Use *any* for plural nouns:

There **aren't any** cars.

2 **Circle the correct words.**

My house is nice. [1] *There's / There are* two bedrooms and [2] *there's / there are* two bathrooms for my family. [3] *There's / There are* a living room, but [4] *there isn't / there aren't* a dining room. [5] *There isn't / There aren't* a yard. My bike is in my bedroom! My favorite place is the kitchen, but [6] *there isn't / there aren't* any pizza today!

3 **Look at the house and complete the sentences with *there's*, *there isn't*, *there are*, and *there aren't*.**

1 ....There's.......... a living room.
2 .... two bedrooms.
3 .... any people in the house.
4 .... a dining room.
5 .... a bathroom.
6 .... two kitchens.

USE IT!

4 **Work in pairs. Give information about your house.**

Tell me about your house.

There are two bedrooms.
There isn't a yard.

LISTENING AND VOCABULARY

1 3.05 **Match the images with the words below. Then listen, check, and repeat.**

• ~~bed~~ • chair • closet • door • shower • table • wall • window

1 

bed

2 

....

3 

....

4 

....

5 

....

6 

....

7 

....

8 

....

2 3.06 **Katia and Maria are on a video call. Listen and check (✓) the correct bedroom.**

1 ◯ 

2 ◯ 

3 3.06 **Listen to the video call again. Circle the correct answers.**

1 **Where is Katia?**
   a in her bedroom b in Julia's bedroom

2 **What color is Katia's chair?**
   a blue b green

3 **Where are Katia's jeans?**
   a on her table b on her bed

4 **Where are Katia's clothes?**
   a in Julia's bedroom b in her bedroom

5 **Who is at the door?**
   a Maria b Julia

LOOK!

The picture is **on** the wall.

The books are **on** the table.

The chair is **in** the living room.

WORKBOOK p.120 and p.121

LANGUAGE IN CONTEXT

1 Complete the questions and answers from the video call in the chart with the words below.

• ~~Is~~ • there is • No • Are there • are

There is/There are	
***Yes/No* questions**	**Short Answers**
___Is___ **there** a picture on the wall?	Yes, ____________ .
Is there a closet?	____________, **there isn't**.
____________ any books?	Yes, **there** ____________ .
Are there any cats in the bedroom?	No, **there aren't**.

2 Put the words in the correct order to make questions.

1 bed / there / a / kitchen / Is / in / the / ?

Is there a bed in the kitchen?

2 your / books / in / Are / bedroom / there / any / ?

____

3 kitchen / a / Is / there / the / table / in / ?

____

4 Are / living /chairs / in / room / the / there / two / ?

____

5 bedroom / closet / there / a / Is / the / in / ?

____

3 Look at this room and answer the questions. Write short answers.

1 Is there a closet?

Yes, there is.

2 Is there a bed?

____

3 Are there two chairs?

____

4 Is there a picture on the wall?

____

5 Are there any windows?

____

USE IT!

4 Check (✓) the objects in your bedroom.

	closet	chair	table	pictures on the wall	window
Me	○	○	○	○	○
My Partner	○	○	○	○	○

5 Work in pairs. Ask and answer questions about your bedrooms. Check (✓) your partner's objects.

Is there a closet in your bedroom?

Yes, there is.

WORKBOOK p.120 and p.122 PRACTICE EXTRA

AROUND THE WORLD

HOME ON WATER

Hello, my name's Leo and I'm from England, in the UK. My home is a houseboat on the River Stort. My friends at school are curious about it because it's on the river, and it's different.

My home is not big, but it's comfortable. There are two bedrooms, a living room, a kitchen, and a bathroom.

There aren't any walls to separate the living room and the kitchen. There's a stove, a fridge, and a small table with chairs. There isn't a sofa, but there are many pictures on the wall and many vases with plants. My parents are fans of nature. There's a TV, too. Oh, and soccer on TV is my favorite thing!

My favorite place at home is my bedroom. In my bedroom, there's a bed, a closet with my comic books and my clothes, a table, and a chair. Ah, and I'm a music student, so of course there's my guitar, too.

And you? What's your home like and what's your favorite place at home?

1 **Look at the text and the images. Then complete the sentences with the words below.**

- magazine • section • title

1 This text is from a ....

2 The name of the .... is *Home Sweet Home.*

3 The .... of the article is *Home on Water.*

2 3.07 **Read and listen to the text and complete the notes.**

1 Leo's country: ....England................

2 Leo's home location: ....

3 Number of rooms in Leo's home: ....

4 Object not present in Leo's home: ....

5 Leo's favorite place at home: ....

WORDS IN CONTEXT

3 **Label the pictures with the words below.**

- river • comic book
- stove • vase

1

................river................

2

....

3

....

4

....

4 **Find the words in the text. Are they similar in your language? Use a dictionary to write the translation.**

1 comfortable ....

2 comic ....

3 curious ....

4 fan ....

5 move ....

5 **Complete the sentences with expressions from the text.**

1 Nature is their favorite thing.

They're ....

2 I'm a sports fan.

Soccer on TV is my ....

6 **Match the causes (1–4) with the consequences (a–d).**

1 Leo's house is different.

2 Soccer on TV is Leo's favorite thing.

3 Leo's parents are fans of nature.

4 Leo's a music student.

a There's a TV in the house. ....

b There's a guitar in his room. ....

c His friends are curious. ....

d There are many vases with plants inside. ....

WEBQUEST

Learn more! Check (✓) *True* or *False*.
Houseboats are only popular in Europe.

○ **True** ○ **False**

THINK!

Are you curious about your friends' homes?
Are they curious about your home? Why?

VIDEO

3.2

1 **What countries do you hear in the video?**

2 **What's your favorite home?**

SPEAKING

REACTING POSITIVELY

1 3.08 **Read and listen to Henry and Layla. Where's Henry?**

Henry Hey, Layla! Look at my **dining room**! Isn't it great?

Layla Oh, wow! What's that? Is it a **table**?

Henry Yes, it is. It's a **Japanese table**. Now look at the **living room**.

Layla What? There aren't any **chairs**!

Henry I know! That's my favorite part of the apartment!

Layla Henry, your new apartment is awesome!

LIVING ENGLISH

2 **Complete the mini dialogues with the expressions below.**

- Isn't it great
- I know
- Oh, wow

1 A This is the yard.
B ______________________!
It's really nice!

2 A Your bedroom's awesome!
B ______________________!
______________________?

3 3.09 **Listen and repeat the expressions.**

PRONUNCIATION

4 3.10 **Listen and repeat.**

Is it a table? ↗

What's that? ↘

5 3.11 **Work in pairs. Read the questions. Then listen and check the pronunciation.**

Is there a yard? ↗

Where's the bedroom? ↘

6 3.08 **Listen to the dialogue again. Then practice with a partner.**

7 **Role play a new dialogue. Follow the steps.**

1 Change the words in blue to write a new dialogue in your notebook.
2 Practice your dialogue with a partner.
3 Present your dialogue to the class.

YOUR DIGITAL PORTFOLIO

Record your dialogue. Then upload it to your class digital portfolio.

PRACTICE EXTRA

4 FAMILY MATTERS

UNIT GOALS

- Talk about people in families.
- Read about different families.
- Listen to two people talking about photos.
- Learn about a family from Brazil.
- Write a description of a family photo.

THINK!

1 What is family?

2 Why is family important?

VIDEO 4.1

1 What are two ways that people in families can be different?

2 Say three reasons why family time is a happy time.

VOCABULARY IN CONTEXT

1 4.01 **Complete Tomas's family tree with the words below. Then listen and check.**

- aunt
- brother
- dad
- ~~grandpa~~
- sister

2 4.02 **Listen and repeat the family words. Then work in pairs. Say the family word and the name.**

grandma

Lucía

3 **Organize the family words in Exercise 1 in the chart below.**

Male	Female	Both
dad	mom	

LOOK!

(informal) grandpa / grandma
(formal) grandfather / grandmother
(informal) dad / mom
(formal) father / mother

4 **Look at the family tree again. Complete the sentences with the words in Exercise 1.**

1 Who's Jaime?
He's Tomas's dad
2 Who's Martin?
He's Catalina's ______.
3 Who's Catalina?
She's Pablo's ______.
4 Who's Antonia?
She's Matias's ______.
5 Who's Jaime?
He's Renata's ______.
6 Who's Lucia?
She's Tomas's ______.
7 Who's Catalina?
She's Matias's ______.

5 **Correct the sentences.**

1 Catalina is Pablo's sister.
No, she's not. She's his cousin.
2 Andrés is Matias's dad.
No, he's not. He's ______.
3 Renata is Tomas's mom.
No, she's not. She's ______.
4 Antonia is Catalina's aunt.
No, she's not. She's ______.
5 Antonia and Jaime are Tomas's grandparents.
No, they're not. They're ______.

USE IT!

6 **Write the names of five people in your family. Then work in pairs. Ask and answer about your partner's family members.**

Who's Sara? Is she your sister?

No, she's my mom. Who's Paolo?

READING

1 Look at the text, the title, and the images. Then check (✓) the correct answer and answer the question.

1 Where are these texts from?
○ a class video presentation ○ a class poster presentation

2 What are these texts about?

OUR FAMILIES

Hi! I'm Josh. This is my house ... and my grandma and grandpa. They're my family. I have a cousin, Alex. Alex's home is in the United Kingdom. He has a big cat, called Suki, but they're not here! So it's my grandpa, my grandma, and me – three of us! Oh, and my two dogs, Pepe and Jaz. They have a small house in the yard! And that's it. We have a small family!

Hi! My name's Zoe. I have a brother, Taylor, but we're from different families: Taylor's dad is not my dad, and my mom is not Taylor's mom. We're a new family and we have a big house – it has four bedrooms! I have a very big family. Taylor has 23 cousins, and I have 11! Together, we have 34 cousins!

2 4.03 Read and listen to the text. Identify Josh and Zoe's families. Write *J* (Josh) or *Z* (Zoe).

1 ------------------------

2 ------------------------

3 Read the text again and circle the correct answers.

1 11 cousins *Josh / Zoe*
2 two dogs *Josh / Zoe*
3 one cousin *Josh / Zoe*
4 a small family *Josh / Zoe*
5 a big family *Josh / Zoe*
6 a grandma and a grandpa *Josh / Zoe*

THINK!
What types of families are there?

WORKBOOK p.127

LANGUAGE IN CONTEXT

1 **Look at the examples below. Complete the sentences from Josh and Zoe's presentations.**

Verb *to have*	
Affirmative (+)	
I, you, we, they	***he, she, it***
I ......have...... a cousin.	**He** .... 23 cousins.
You have a sister.	
We .... 34 cousins!	**She has** a brother.
They .... a small house in the yard!	**It** .... four bedrooms.

2 **Circle the correct verbs.**

1 My brother and I (*have*) / *has* a big family.
2 Mira *have* / *has* a brother called Sergio.
3 I *have* / *has* ten aunts and uncles, but I only *have* / *has* two cousins.
4 My friend Sam *have* / *has* two sisters and they *have* / *has* a dog.
5 They're a big family and they *have* / *has* a big house. It *have* / *has* seven bedrooms.

LOOK!
There are five people in my family.
I **have** two sisters.

3 **Look at the images and write sentences. Use *has* or *have* and the words below.**

• ~~a sister~~ • a brother • two cousins • a grandpa • a grandma

1

Leo and Felix ...have a sister....

2

He ....

3

We ....

4

Nina ....

5

I ....

USE IT!

I have eight cousins.

4 **Write three sentences about your family. Read them to your partner.**

5 **Write sentences about your partner's family. Read them to the class.**

Maria has eight cousins.
....
....

WORKBOOK p.124 and p.126 PRACTICE EXTRA

LISTENING AND VOCABULARY

1 4.04 **Label the images with the words below. Then listen, check, and repeat.**

- blue eyes
- long hair
- brown eyes
- ~~short~~
- dark hair
- short hair
- fair hair
- tall
- green eyes

1 short

2 ....

3 ....

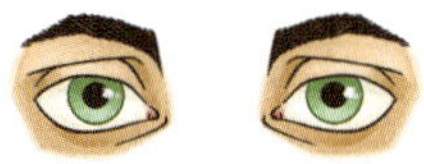

4 ....

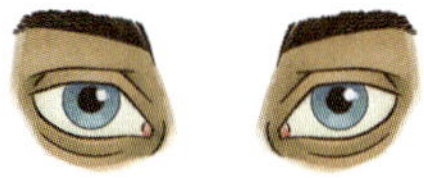

5 ....

6 ....

7 ....

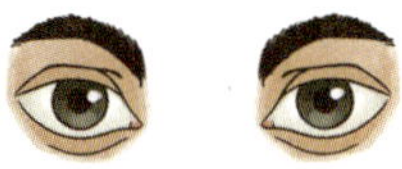

8 ....

9 ....

2 4.05 **Listen to Mariana and Larissa and write the names of the people in the pictures.**

- Luciana
- Helena
- Antonio
- Gabi
- Eduardo

1 ....

2 ....

3 ....

3 **Look at your answers above and complete the sentence.**

There are .... people in Mariana's family.

4 4.05 **Listen to Mariana and Larissa again and check (✓) the words that describe the people in the photos.**

	brown eyes	tall	short	fair hair	dark hair	long hair
Luciana	○	○	✓	○	○	○
Antonio	○	○	○	○	○	○
Gabi	○	○	○	○	○	○
Helena	○	○	○	○	○	○
Eduardo	○	○	○	○	○	○

WORKBOOK p.124 and p.125

LANGUAGE IN CONTEXT

1 **Complete the questions and answers from the dialogue in the chart. Use the words below.**

• ~~Do~~ • Does • doesn't • I do • she does

Verb *to have* (*I*, *you*, *he*, *she*, *we*, *they*)		
Negative (-)	***Yes/No* Questions**	**Short Answers**
I **don't have** a sister	**Do** I **have** a sister?	No, I **don't**.
You **don't have** the photo.	Do you **have** the photo?	Yes, ______
He/She **doesn't have** blue eyes.	______ he/she **have** blue eyes?	No, he/she ______
We **don't have** long hair.	**Do** we **have** long hair?	Yes, we **do**.
They **don't have** green eyes.	**Do** they **have** green eyes?	No, they **don't**.

2 **Circle the correct verbs to complete the sentences.**

1 I ______ a big family. It's my dad, my mom, and me.
a have b don't have

2 My mom ______ a sister. Her name is Sarah.
a has b doesn't have

3 My cousins and I ______ green eyes. They're blue!
a have b don't have

4 My dad ______ any brothers or sisters.
a has b doesn't have

LOOK!
My family has seven members.
BUT
There are seven members in my family.

3 **Put the words in the correct order to make questions. Then answer them.**

1 have / Does / dark / Isabella / hair / ? (X)
Does Isabella have dark hair? No, she doesn't.

2 you / eyes, George / Do / brown / have / ? (✓)
______ ______

3 any / Michael / have / Does / cousins / ? (X)
______ ______

4 Do / Alicia and Florence / long / have / hair / ? (X)
______ ______

USE IT!

4 **Complete the questions and answer them so they are true for you. Mark (✓) or (X).**

	Me	My Partner
Do you have dark hair?	○	○
______ you have long hair?	○	○
______ your mom have a brother or a sister?	○	○
______ your dad have brown eyes?	○	○

5 **Work in pairs. Ask and answer the questions. Mark (✓) or (X) in the chart for your partner.**

WORKBOOK p.124 and p.126 PRACTICE EXTRA

ACROSS THE CURRICULUM

MATH

The Saraíba Family

By João Miguel Saraíba
6th Grade
Teacher: Mrs. Capanema.

Who are we?

We're a happy Brazilian family from the Amazon!

In my house, it's just my mom, my grandparents, my dog, and me. It's not a very big family. But I have three uncles, and four aunts. My aunt Janaína is single. My other uncles and aunts are all married, and I have many cousins.

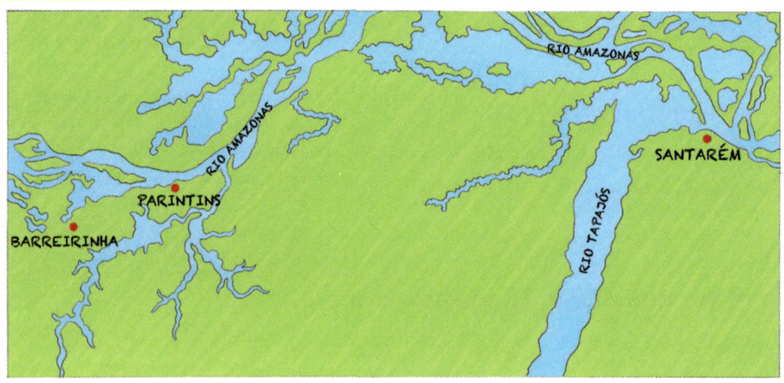

I have 20 cousins. Six are from Parintins, like me, and four are from Barreirinha. My other cousins are from Santarém. All my cousins have brothers and sisters, but I don't. I'm an only child, but it's OK. I have my dog, Cupuaçu. That's the name of my favorite fruit, too.

My dog and me

My cousin Uiara and me

Cupuaçu fruit

We love parties!

My uncle Murici and my aunt Jacira have a big house in Paritins with cupuaçu and pupunha trees in the yard. We have family celebrations there.

All our relatives and friends love our parties. We really have fun together, with a lot of Amazon food and music. And, of course, birthday cakes!

My aunt Jacira and her birthday cake

1 **Look at João Miguel's poster. Who is the audience? Check (✓) the correct answer.**

- ◯ João Miguel's family
- ◯ Mrs. Capanema and the students in his class
- ◯ the teacher and his mom
- ◯ young people on the Internet

2 4.06 **Read and listen to the poster. Write *T* (true) or *F* (false) next to the statements.**

1. 1/4 of João Miguel's cousins are from Parintins. ....
2. 50% of João Miguel's cousins are from Santarém. ....
3. João Miguel has 19 cousins. ....
4. The cousins from Barreirinha have three brothers and sisters. ....
5. One cousin from Santarém is an only child. ....

3 **Where are João Miguel's cousins from? Check (✓) the correct chart.**

◯ 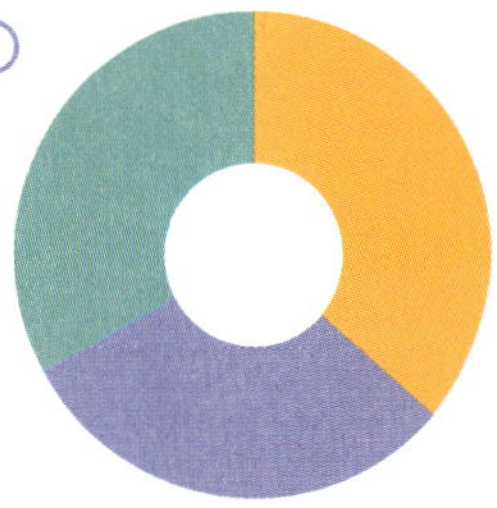

◯ 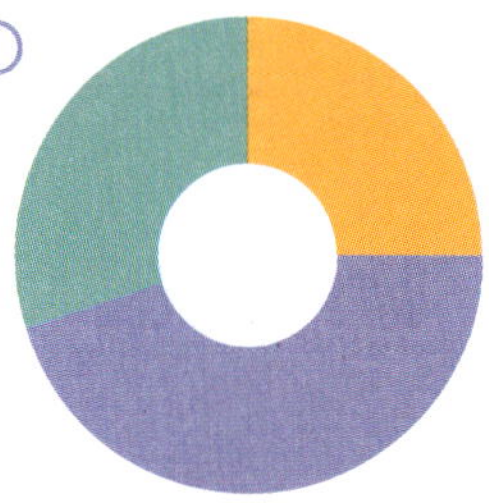

◯ 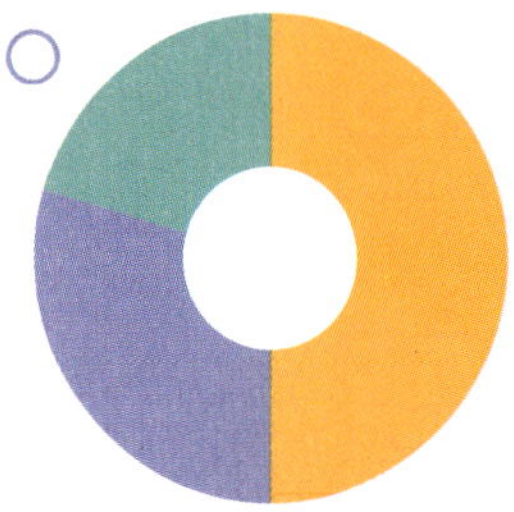

- Barreirinhas
- Parintins
- Santarém

4 **Read the poster again and answer the questions.**

1. Where in Brazil is João Miguel's family from?
   the Amazon
2. Is João Miguel's dog part of the family?
   ....
3. What is João Miguel's favorite fruit?
   ....
4. Where are the family's celebrations?
   ....
5. What is there at the parties?
   ....

WORDS IN CONTEXT

5 **Match the words (1–4) with the definitions (a–d).**

1 only child	a celebration
2 party	b family members
3 single	c not married
4 relatives	d person with no brothers or sisters

WEBQUEST

Learn more! Check (✓) *True* or *False*. About 30% of Brazilian families have a grandparent in the same house.

◯ **True** ◯ **False**

THINK!

Are your friends part of your family? Why / Why not?

VIDEO

4.2

1. **Where in the world are there big families?**
2. **Where in the world are there small families?**

WRITING

1 **Look at the text. What is it? Check (✓) the correct answer.**

◯ an email to a pen pal ◯ an online magazine article

16: 54

Bruno
to me
at 4:20 PM

Hi!

I'm Bruno. I'm tall and I have fair hair and green eyes, and this is my family. My mom is tall and has long, dark hair. My dad is tall, too. He has long, fair hair and brown eyes. Their names are Amanda and Isaac. My little sister is next to my mom. Her name's Leticia. She's short and has short, brown hair. Oh, my grandma Clara is not in the photo because she's the photographer!

2 4.07 **Read and listen to the text. Write the name of each person in Bruno's family. Then complete the chart.**

Me!	Bruno
mom	
	Isaac
sister	
	Clara

LOOK!

He has **long**, **fair** hair.
She has **short**, **brown** hair.
Order of adjectives: style, color

3 **Write your description of your family to a pen pal.**

1 Include a photo.
2 Introduce yourself.
3 Describe the people in the photo.

4 **Switch your description with a partner and check his/her work. Use the checklist.**

◯ photo
◯ information about the people
◯ order of adjectives

YOUR DIGITAL PORTFOLIO

Edit your description. Then publish it. Upload it to the class portfolio for everyone to see!

REVIEW
UNITS 3 AND 4

VOCABULARY

1 **Look at the image. Number the parts of the house.**

.... bathroom .... dining room
.... bedroom ....1.... kitchen
.... living room .... yard

2 **Look at the Oliveira's family tree. Check (✓) the correct sentences. Then correct the wrong one.**

1 Juliana is Luis and Paula's sister. ◯
2 Leonardo is Henrique's dad. ◯
3 Mauro is Vitor's grandpa. ◯
4 Sandra is Ingrid's grandma. ◯

....

3 **Look at the images and circle the correct words to complete the sentences.**

1 Eliana has *brown* / *green* eyes.

2 Luciana has *short* / *long* hair.

3 Jacob has *blue* / *green* eyes.

4 A Is Francisco *short* / *tall*?
B Yes, he is.

4 **Look at Nadia's house and complete the sentences with *There's*, *There isn't*, *There are*, and *There aren't*.**

1 .... any chairs in the kitchen.
2 .... a window in the bedroom.
3 .... a closet in the bedroom.
4 .... pictures in the bathroom.

LANGUAGE IN CONTEXT

5 **Complete the questions about Nadia's house. Then answer them.**

1 Is there ______ a table in the kitchen?
No, there isn't. ______

2 ______ any chairs in the living room? ______

3 ______ a TV in the living room? ______

4 ______ any windows in the bathroom? ______

6 **Write questions with the verb *to have*. Then answer them.**

1 Luciano / a brother and two sisters? (✓)
Does Luciano have a brother and two sisters? Yes, he does.

2 You / a dog and a cat? (**X**)
______

3 We / six uncles and eight aunts? (✓)
______

4 Your dad / sister called / Debora? (**X**)
______

7 **Complete the dialogue with the words below.**

• are there • do • has • ~~have~~ • there are • there aren't • there's

Tomas Do you [1] have ______ a big house?

Priscilla Yes, I [2] ______. My family is big. [3] ______ five bedrooms in my house: one for my dad and my mom, one for my sisters Ana and Beatriz, one for me and my sister Juliana, and one for my brother Tiago.

Tomas Wait … that's four bedrooms.

Priscilla Oh, right. [4] ______ a bedroom for my grandma. And she [5] ______ two cats, Lola and Nikita.

Tomas [6] ______ any dogs in your house?

Priscilla No, [7] ______.

CHECK YOUR PROGRESS

I CAN...

- **talk about parts of the house and furniture.** 🙂 ○ 🙁 ○
- **use *there is*/*there are* to describe a home or a part of a house.** 🙂 ○ 🙁 ○
- **talk about my family and their physical descriptions.** 🙂 ○ 🙁 ○
- **use the verb *to have* to talk about my family.** 🙂 ○ 🙁 ○

LEARN TO LEARN

It's very important to look at new words every day. Write the new words from your class on small pieces of paper and put them in a jar. Choose one word from the jar every day, read it, and remember it!

5 A DAY IN THE LIFE

UNIT GOALS

- Talk about your daily routine.
- Read a page from a student's blog.
- Listen to a podcast.
- Learn about life in a circus.
- Talk about your free time.

THINK!

1 What's important in the girl's daily routine?

2 What's important in your daily routine?

VIDEO

5.1

Name the countries in the video. Are daily routines similar around the world?

VOCABULARY IN CONTEXT

1 5.01 **Complete Ivory's video captions with the expressions below. Then listen and check your answers.**

- do my homework
- ~~get up~~
- go home
- go to bed
- go to school
- have breakfast
- have dinner
- play volleyball
- take a shower
- take the bus

My Daily Routine!

1

On school days, I ____get up____ at 6:00.

2

At 6:30, I ______________________ with my family.

3

At 7:00, I ______________________ with my brother. We ______________________.

4

I ______________________ on Mondays and Wednesdays. These are my favorite days!

5

I ______________ at 4:00 and I ______________ ______________.

6

Then I ______________________.

7

I ______________________ with my brother and my mom.

8

Finally, I ______________________.

2 **Complete the chart with the expressions in Exercise 1.**

In the morning	**In** the afternoon	**In** the evening	**At** night
	play volleyball		

3 **Complete the chart with the expressions.**

- a pizza
- ~~the bus~~
- a shower
- the subway
- breakfast
- to bed
- home
- to school

take: the train, ..., ..., the bus

have: a hamburger, ..., ...

go: ...., ..., ...

USE IT!

4 5.02 **Listen and read. Check (✓) the sentences that are true for you.**

	Me	My Partner
I do homework in the afternoon.		
I get up at 6:00 on Mondays.		
I have dinner with my family.		
I have lunch at 1:00.		
I take a shower in the morning.		
I take the bus to school.		

Work in pairs. Tell your partner your true sentences. Check (✓) the sentences your partner says.

What's your favorite time of day? Why?

My favorite time of day is morning.

READING

www.fresheyesfromsingapore.net

Fresh Eyes
FROM SINGAPORE

HOME | ABOUT | PICTURES | SCHOOL

Hi! My name is Wei Jie, and I'm 14.

I'm a student from Singapore. My passion is photography. I get up at 5:30 and I have breakfast. Then I take the MRT train to school with my friend Teo. Lessons start at 8:10, but before class, we work on math exercises. We finish school at 2:15. I don't play sports. When I go home, I have lunch but I don't rest. I do my homework and study until 8:00. Then I take a shower and have dinner with my parents. They ask a lot of questions! I chat online with friends. Then I study more. I like to watch TV series, but I don't have time for that.

I go to bed at 10:00. On Sundays, I don't study! I take photos in the city and post them on my blog. I hope you like my photos!

Sri Mariamman Temple

Singapore Mass Rapid Transport (MRT)

Shopping Mall

1 **Look at the titles, images and design. Then answer the questions.**

1 What type of text is this?
   ◯ an "about me" page on a blog   ◯ a student's school file
2 Who is the author? ....
3 What is her hobby? ....

2 5.03 **Read and listen to the text and put the activities in chronological order.**

.... We work on math exercises.
.... I go home.
.... I do homework and study.
.... I chat online.
.... I have lunch.
.... I take a shower.
.... I go to bed.
.... We finish school.

3 **Write *T* (true) or *F* (false) next to the statements for Wei Jie.**

My Daily Routine	Wei Jie	Me
1 I study a lot!		
2 I go to school with a friend.		
3 I watch TV in the evening.		
4 I don't do math in the morning.		
5 I don't play sports on weekdays.		
6 I don't have dinner with my parents.		

4 **What about you? Write *T* (true) or *F* (false) next to the statements for you.**

THINK!

School and homework are a big part of Wei Jie's day. Is it good to study a lot like Wei Jie? Why? / Why not?

WORKBOOK p.131

LANGUAGE IN CONTEXT

1 **Look at the examples in the chart. Complete the sentences from Wei Jie's blog.**

Simple Present (*I, you, we, they*)	
Affirmative (+)	**Negative (-)**
I ...get up... at 5:30.	On Sundays, I ...don't... study!
I .... to bed at 10:00.	I .... play sports.
You **do** your homework.	You **don't do** your homework.
They .... a lot of questions!	They **don't ask** a lot of questions.
We .... school at 2:15.	We **don't finish** school at 4:00.

LOOK!

at | 8:00 p.m.
| 10:15 a.m.

on | Monday
| Tuesday
| the weekend / weekdays

2 **Complete the sentences with the affirmative (+) or negative (-) forms of the verbs in parentheses.**

1 We ...don't take... (take) the bus to school. We walk. (-)
2 I .... (have) lunch at school, then I go home. (+)
3 We .... (take) a shower in the morning. (+)
4 They .... (play) sports on weekdays. (-)
5 You .... (watch) TV in the evenings. (-)

3 **Make true sentences about your routine. Write the affirmative (+) or negative (-) forms of the verbs.**

• take • chat • take • ~~get up~~ • have • get up

1 I ...get up... at 5:30 on weekdays.
2 I .... at 5:30 on Sundays.
3 I .... the bus to school on Saturdays.
4 I .... a shower in the evening.
5 My parents .... dinner with me in the evening.
6 My friends and I .... online on weekends.

USE IT!

4 **Work in pairs. Give information that is true for you.**

I don't get up at 5:30 on weekdays. What about you?

I don't get up at 5:30 on weekdays. I get up at 6:30.

LISTENING AND VOCABULARY

1 **Look at the image and check (✓) the correct answers.**

1 **What does it represent?**
- ◯ an interview with a boy named Ramiro
- ◯ a song by Ramiro Bolaños

2 **What's the topic of the podcast with Ramiro?**
- ◯ study life
- ◯ weekend activities

2 🔊 **5.04 Listen to the podcast and check your answers.**

3 🔊 **5.05 Listen to the first part of the podcast again and circle the correct options.**

1 Ramiro is *12 / 13* years old.
2 He is from *Guatemala / the USA*.
3 Ramiro lives in *Jalapa / Boston*.
4 Ramiro's weekends are *fun / boring*.

4 🔊 **5.06 Listen to the rest of the podcast and check (✓) Ramiro's free-time activities.**

1
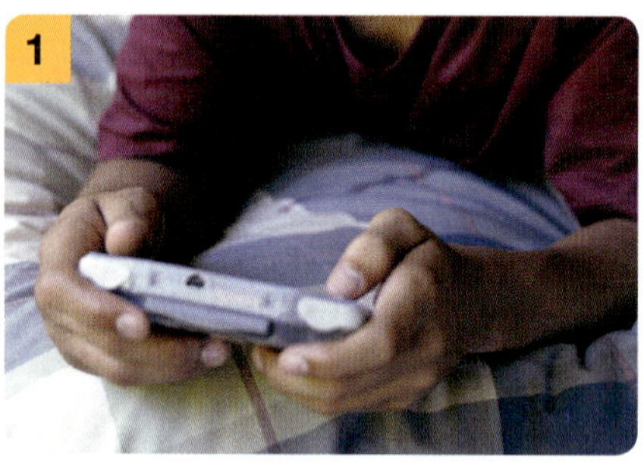
◯ play video games

2

◯ watch movies

3

◯ play soccer

4

◯ listen to music

5

◯ hang out with friends

6

◯ go to restaurants

WORKBOOK p.128 and p.129

LANGUAGE IN CONTEXT

1 **Complete the chart with the words below.**

• do • do • do • don't • don't • ~~play~~ • what

Simple Present (*I, you, we, they*)	
***Yes/No* Questions**	**Short Answers**
Do you ......play...... soccer on Sundays? **Do** you **play** sports? .... they **watch** TV on weekends? .... they **take** the subway to school?	Yes, I **do**. No, I .... Yes, they **do**. No, they ....
***Wh-* Questions**	**Answers**
What .... you **do** on weekends? .... time **do** you **get up**? **Where do** they **have** lunch?	I **play** volleyball and **hang out** with friends. I **get up** at 9:00 on weekends. They **have** lunch at home.

2 **Read the answers. Then put the words in the correct order to make questions.**

1 your / homework / lunch / you / Do / do / after / ?

....

Yes, I do. I study for an hour.

2 shower / Do / a / take / in / you / morning / the / ?

....

No, I don't. I take a shower in the evening.

3 lunch / for / What / have / you / do / ?

....

I have pizza.

4 do / Where / they / go / Sundays / on / ?

....

They go to their grandparents' house.

USE IT!

3 **Complete the questions and answer with information about you.**

1 What do you .... on weekday evenings? I ....
....

2 Do you .... in the morning? ....
....

3 Where .... on weekends? I ....
....

4 **Work in pairs. Ask and answer the questions.**

AROUND THE WORLD

www.globalyouth.com

GLOBAL YOUTH

NEWS SPORTS THE ARTS MAKE A DIFFERENCE PROFILES COMMENTS

Circus Life!

by maxpadu | 9:50, July 10

Hi! I'm Anna, and I'm 14. I'm always in the air and on the road!

I'm from Prague, the capital of the Czech Republic. I live in a trailer with my little brother Jan and our parents. Our trailer is part of a big circus caravan. We travel around Europe, and home is where the heart is!

I don't go to a regular school. My brother and I take classes with my parents in the morning. I have an online tutor, too. I also have a place in the trailer to study and keep my things.

In the afternoon, I hang out with my friends in the circus and I practice my skills. I don't have friends outside the caravan, but it's OK. I meet new people in every town we stop in.

I do juggling and aerial acrobatics. I practice seven days a week for four hours, but I don't mind because I love acrobatics.

In the evening, we do our show. Mom, Dad, Jan, and I do a family act together. I like my life because we're free, and we do what we love.

ONLINE COMMENTS

Bunnie the bear
Do you have animals in your circus? I hope not! It's cruel.

reply share

Edward
Hello. You don't go to school? That's so cool!!

reply share

preet preet
Circuses are creepy 😱. I don't know if it's the clowns, or the music … I never go.

reply share

Your Comment:

POST

1 **Look at the text. Check (✓) all the elements that you see.**

- ◯ a logo
- ◯ a title
- ◯ comments
- ◯ date
- ◯ headings for different parts of the text
- ◯ images

2 **A text with these elements is probably …**

- ◯ an online article.
- ◯ an online forum.
- ◯ an opinion article in a book.

3 5.07 **Where is Anna from? Read and listen to the text. Check your answers.**

4 **Anna says, "I'm always in the air and on the road." Why?**

- ◯ Anna and her family fly to different places to do their show.
- ◯ Anna is part of a circus family and she and her family travel a lot.

5 **What is it possible to say, based on the text? Check (✓) the correct answers.**

1 **Friends**
- ◯ Anna and her friends spend time together.
- ◯ Anna is not happy because all her friends are from the circus.

2 **Education**
- ◯ Anna's parents are responsible for her education.
- ◯ People in the circus don't study regularly.

3 **Work**
- ◯ Anna and her family don't work on weekends.
- ◯ Anna and her family work together in the circus.

WORDS IN CONTEXT

6 **Match the expressions in the text (1–2) with their definitions (a–b).**

1 I practice my skills.
2 I hang out with my friends.
a I work on circus activities. ....
b I spend time with boys and girls. ....

THINK!

1 **Read the online comments. Write your opinion about the article in the space below "Your Comment".**

2 **In your opinion, what's the meaning of this sentence from the article: "Home is where the heart is"?**

....
....
....
....

WEBQUEST

Learn more! Check (✓) *True* or *False*. The famous *Cirque du Soleil* use animals in their shows.

◯ True ◯ False

VIDEO

5.2

1 **I'm Mya. What time do I go to school?**
2 **What do I do in the evening?**

SPEAKING

A CLASS SURVEY

1 5.08 **Read and listen to Amelia and Noah.**

Amelia Hi, Noah! What do you do on **Saturday afternoons?**
Noah I **play basketball** with my friends.
Amelia Do you go out with your **family**?
Noah Yes, I do. We go to **the park** or a **museum**.
Amelia Really?!? Do you like **museums**?
Noah Sure! How about you?
Amelia **No way!**

LIVING ENGLISH

- Sure!
- Really?
- No way!

2 **Which expressions do they use to ...**

1 show surprise? ....
2 say yes? ....
3 say no? ....

3 5.09 **Listen and repeat the expressions.**

PRONUNCIATION

Linking sounds: do you /dju/

4 5.10 **Listen and repeat.**

Do you go out with your family?

And **what do you** do on Saturday afternoons?

5 5.08 **Listen to the dialogue again. Then practice with a partner.**

6 **Tell people about your free time activities. Follow the steps.**

1 Change the words in **blue** to write a new dialogue in your notebook.
2 Practice your dialogue with a partner.
3 Present your dialogue to the class.

YOUR DIGITAL PORTFOLIO

Record your dialogue. Then upload it to your class digital portfolio.

PRACTICE EXTRA

6 SCHOOL TIME

UNIT GOALS

- Talk about school.
- Read school notices.
- Listen to a school radio program.
- Learn about the planets in the solar system.
- Write a class presentation.

THINK!

1 Is your school similar to the one in the photo? Why / Why not?

2 Why is education important?

VIDEO

6.1

1 Which two things in the video do all students do at school?

2 List five types of places from the video where students study.

VOCABULARY IN CONTEXT

1 6.01 **Look at Olivia's schedule and listen. What's Olivia's favorite subject?**

....

2 6.01 **Listen again and complete the schedule with the words below.**

• history • math • music • ~~PE~~ • science • Spanish

SCHOOL SUBJECTS				
		Monday	Tuesday	Wednesday
Morning	8:10–9:15	PE	art	....
	9:20–10:25	PE	art	....
	10:25–10:40	BREAK		
	10:40–11:45	science	English	....
	11:45–12:30	LUNCH		
Afternoon	12:30–1:35	geography	English	....
	1:40–2:45	geography	....	computer science
	2:45–3:30	....	....	computer science
	3:45–4:55	SPORTS CLUB	SCIENCE CLUB	ART CLUB

3 6.02 **Number the subjects in the order you hear them from 1–10. Then listen again, check, and repeat.**

.... math
.... English
.... Spanish
.... science
.... computer science
.... music
.... art
.... history
.... geography
.... PE

4 6.03 **Listen to the sounds. What's the subject? What day is it?**

1 math Wednesday
2 ....
3 ....
4 ....
5 ....

5 Look at the school subjects and draw a face (*like*, *love*, *don't like*, *hate*) for you.

LIKE 🙂 LOVE 🙂🙂 DON'T LIKE 🙁 HATE 🙁🙁

Subject	Me	My Partner
math		
art		
history		
PE		
geography		

Subject	Me	My Partner
science		
music		
Spanish		
English		

6 Look at the images. Write sentences with *love*, *like*, *don't like*, and *hate*.

1 🙂🙂

I <u>love science.</u>

2 🙁🙁

You ....

3 🙁

I ....

4 🙂

We ....

5 🙁

You ....

USE IT!

7 Work in pairs. Ask and answer questions to complete the chart in Exercise 5 for your partner. Compare your answers.

Do you like PE?

No, I don't! I hate PE!

Do you like history?

Yes, I do!

WORKBOOK p.133 PRACTICE EXTRA

READING

1 **Look at the image below. Check (✓) the information you can find.**

- ✓ days of the week
- ○ teachers' names
- ○ places at school
- ○ students' names
- ○ school subjects
- ○ room number
- ○ time
- ○ school name

2 **Look at the word in italics. What is it? Circle the correct option.**

It's a school *bulletin board / newspaper*.

A

ATTENTION!
All Science Students
Mr. Rothmann doesn't teach science in a normal way – he works with projects! Come to the Science Project on Friday at 8 a.m.
Don't forget your lab clothes!

B

MUSIC CLASS
Come and listen to the band.

When? Wednesday
What time? 4 p.m.
Where? The music classroom

Linda plays the guitar.
Klaus plays the drums.
Alec doesn't play an instrument, but he's a good singer!

C

ARE YOU A DOG OR A CAT FAN?

Come and help at the animal center! Craig, from 10th grade, helps at the animal center on Saturdays.

More information?
Contact
Craig Clinton
in Room 23,
every day at 3 p.m.

D

Problems with math?
Come and visit Hannah, our math expert.
On Tuesdays, she's in Classroom 6 from 3 p.m. to 4 p.m.
She studies with students and teaches them practical math tips.
Become a math expert, like Hannah!

E

SALE!
Each backpack costs $10!
All colors, all designs.
To order your new backpack, write to me at patibothamm@memail.com or text me at 555-9436.

3 🔊 **6.04 Read and listen to the texts. Which of the texts is good for the people below? Write the letters (A–E).**

1 Ruben has problems with algebra. ....
2 Carol doesn't have a school bag. ....
3 Tom has new lab clothes. ....
4 Nozomi is at school at 4 p.m. on Wednesday. ....
5 Jenny has a cat and is free on Saturdays. ....

4 **Read the texts again and correct the sentences.**

1 Mr. Rothmann is a music teacher.
Mr. Rothmann is a science teacher.
2 The science project is on Thursday.
....
3 The music class is at 5 p.m.
....
4 The backpacks are $15.
....
5 Hannah is a math student.
....
6 Craig is at the animal center every day.
....

THINK!

1 What is the ideal schedule for you?
2 Write about your dream day at school.

WORKBOOK p.135

LANGUAGE IN CONTEXT

1 **Look at the examples in the chart. Complete the sentences from the bulletin board.**

Simple Present (*he*, *she*, *it*)	
Affirmative (+)	**Negative (-)**
Linda **plays** the guitar.	Alec **doesn't** ....play.... an instrument.
Craig .... at the animal center.	Mr. Rothmann .... **teach** science in a normal way.
Hannah .... with students.	She **doesn't study** on Mondays.
Each backpack .... $10.	The backpack **doesn't cost** $20.

2 **Circle the correct verbs to complete the sentences.**

1 Hannah doesn't .... to Classroom 6 on Saturdays.
a go (circled) b goes

2 Klaus .... in the band.
a play b plays

3 Mr. Rothmann .... to Classroom 2 for the science project on Friday.
a go b goes

4 Pati .... colored backpacks.
a sell b sells

5 Hannah doesn't .... English
a teach b teaches

LOOK!

read – read**s**
sell – sell**s**
play – play**s**
stay – stay**s**
teach – teach**es**
go – go**es**
study – stud**ies**

3 **Complete the sentences. Use the correct form of the verbs.**

1 Craig ....stays.... (stay) in Room 23 at 3 p.m.
2 Klaus .... (not read) at 4 p.m. on Wednesday.
3 Lisa .... (study) with Hannah in Classroom 6.
4 Alec .... (not play) guitar.
5 Pati .... (not sell) old backpacks.
6 Craig .... (help) at the animal center.

USE IT!

4 **Work in pairs. Ask and answer questions about school. Mark (✓) or (X) in the chart.**

	My Partner
get up at 7 a.m. on school days	○
have English class every day	○
go to school on Saturday	○
hate math	○
love geography	○
like music	○

Do you get up at 7 a.m. on school days?

No, I don't. / Yes, I do.

5 **Use the information in Exercise 4 to write a short description of your partner.**

Molly gets up at 7 a.m. on school days. She ...

WORKBOOK p.132 and p.134 PRACTICE EXTRA

LISTENING AND VOCABULARY

1 6.05 **Listen to a school radio program. What is it about? Check (✓) the correct option.**

◯ new popular songs ◯ school activities ◯ new teachers

2 6.05 **Listen to the school radio program again. Number the school places below (1–9) with the diagram.**

(7) athletic field ◯ cafeteria ◯ gymnasium ◯ library ◯ maker lab
◯ principal's office ◯ restrooms ◯ science lab ◯ teachers' lounge

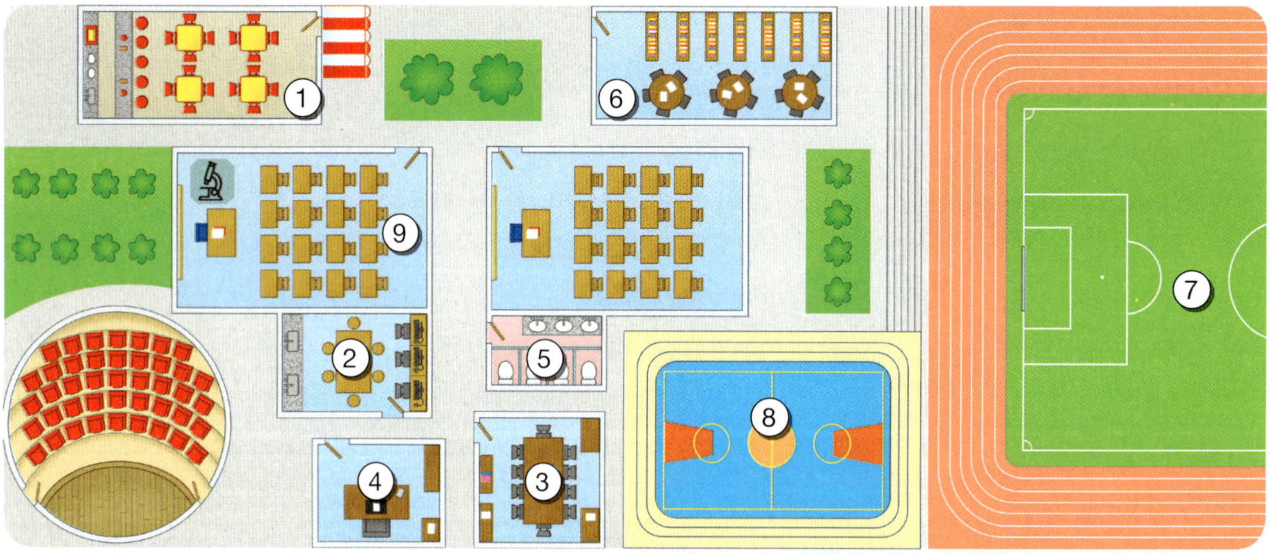

3 6.06 **Listen, check, and repeat.**

4 6.05 **Listen again and match the beginnings of the sentences (1–5) with the endings (a–e).**

1 Aaron is in the
2 Students work with robots in the
3 The maker lab is by the
4 Read your favorite authors in the
5 Soccer practice is at the

a maker lab.
b athletic field.
c teachers' lounge.
d cafeteria.
e library.

THINK!

1 Do you have a school radio station in your school?
2 Is it a good idea to have one? Why? / Why not?

WORKBOOK p.132 and p.133

LANGUAGE IN CONTEXT

1 **Complete the questions and answers from the radio program in the chart. Use the words below.**

• Does • Does • does • does • doesn't • ~~have~~

Simple Present (*he, she, it*)	
***Yes/No* Questions**	**Short Answers**
________ he **speak**?	No, he ________.
Does she **like** robots?	Yes, she **does**.
________ it ____have____ a 3-D printer?	Yes, it ________.
***Wh-* Questions**	**Answers**
Where does he **do** projects?	He **does** projects in the maker lab.
When ________ it **open**?	It **opens** at 8 a.m.
What does the library **have**?	It **has** books!

LOOK!

In English, there is always a subject in the sentence.

What time does your class start?

It starts at 7:10. (The class starts at 7:10).

2 **Answer the questions.**

1 A Does Grayson ride his bike to school?
B __No, he doesn't. He takes__ the bus.

2 A Does Kaylee watch videos before bed?
B No, ________ ________. She ________ books.

3 A Does Amelia have lunch at the school cafeteria?
B No, ________ ________. She ________ lunch at home.

4 A Does Elijah take science lab classes?
B Yes, ________ ________.

3 **Write questions.**

1 Maria / like / robots
__Does Maria like robots?__

2 Zak / get up / at six o'clock / on weekends
____

3 Clara / chat online / in the morning
____

4 Eliot / take the bus / to school / every day
____

USE IT!

What do you do in the evening?

I play volleyball.

4 **Complete the chart so it is true for you. Then work in pairs. Ask and answer the questions and complete the chart with your partner's answers.**

	Me	**My Partner**
What do / in the evening		
have math / Tuesday		
Where go / after school		

5 **Switch partners. Ask and answer the questions about different students.**

Does Maria have math on Tuesday?

Yes, she does.

WORKBOOK p.132 and p.134

ACROSS THE CURRICULUM

SCIENCE

www.highlight.com

Highlight

What do you know about **Jupiter**?

By Mia Stone

Marvin Oatsmann from 7th grade is our school's participant in this year's National Science Fair in Baltimore. Read the interview and learn more about Marvin and his work.

Congratulations, Marvin! Do you participate every year in our school's science fair?

Thanks! Yes, I do! I think participation is very important. I'm crazy about science classes.

Your work this year is about Jupiter. Why?

Well, I like everything about the solar system and the planets, and Jupiter is a very special planet. It's a gas giant made of hydrogen and helium.

Is it possible to see Jupiter from Earth?

Sure! When you look at the sky at night you see the moon, you see Venus, and you see Jupiter, too!

That's fantastic! What other things are interesting about Jupiter?

Oh, so many things ... Jupiter has 79 moons, and it has rings, too, similar to the rings of Saturn. And there's the Great Red Spot, a great storm in the atmosphere of the planet.

Wow, awesome! Thank you, Marvin, and good luck at the National Science Fair!

Thank you!

1 **Look at the text title, design, and images. What type of text is it? Check (✓) the correct answer.**

- ◯ a blog post
- ◯ an interview in a newspaper
- ◯ a discussion in an online forum

2 **Read the title. What is the main topic of the text? Check (✓) the correct answer.**

- ◯ a description of the planets
- ◯ how to participate in a science fair
- ◯ information about Jupiter

3 6.07 **Read and listen to the text. Check (✓) the correct answers.**

1 **Marvin Oatsmann ...**
- ◯ studies in a school in Baltimore.
- ◯ likes 7th grade science classes very much.

2 **Marvin's work ...**
- ◯ is about Jupiter's moons.
- ◯ represents his school in the National Science Fair.

3 **The school science fair ...**
- ◯ happens every year at the school.
- ◯ is about Jupiter this year.

4 **Read the text again and answer the questions.**

1 What do you see in the sky at night?

____

2 Does Jupiter have 77 moons?

____

3 What is the Great Red Spot?

____

4 Does Saturn have rings?

____

WORDS IN CONTEXT

5 **Respond to the statements with the expressions below.**

- Congratulations!
- Good luck!

A I have a difficult soccer game on Friday at school. I hope we win.

____

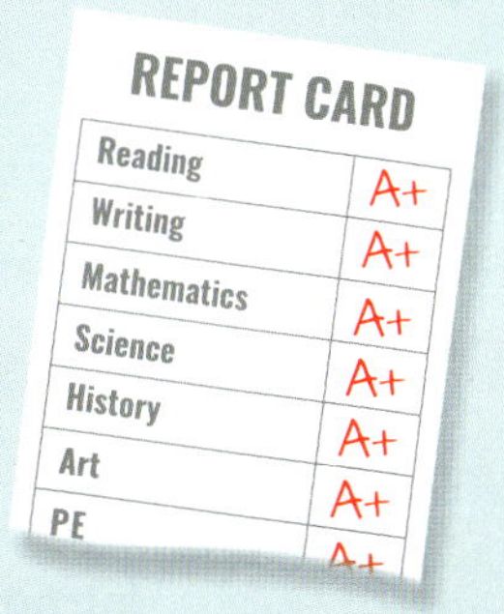

B My report card this year has ten 'A's.

____

6 **Find expressions in the text that are similar to the expressions below.**

1 severe weather, like a tornado or hurricane _______________
2 I really like ... _______________
3 Of course! _______________

WEBQUEST

Learn more! What are the names of the eight planets in the solar system?

THINK!

1 **Is there a science fair in your school? Do you participate? Why / Why not?**

2 **What are you crazy about at school?**

VIDEO

6.2

1 How many planets are in our solar system?
2 Which planet is really hot?

WRITING

LOOK!

In the presentations, use icons to help people understand your message.

1 6.08 **Read and listen to the presentation. Answer the questions.**

1 **How many words are there on each slide?**

Slide 1: 3 Slide 2: ...... Slide 3: ......

Slide 4: ...... Slide 5: ...... Slide 6: ......

2 **Do the images represent the ideas in the text?**

....

2 Put the slide numbers in the correct place in the chart.

Title	Introduction	Information	Conclusion
Slide 1			

3 Read the *Look!* box. Think of another icon.

4 Plan a presentation about your ideal school.

1 **Think about the subjects you study and the places in a school.**

2 **Collect images to illustrate the presentation.**

3 **Make short notes on each slide.**

4 **Write the first version of your presentation.**

5 Switch presentations with a partner and check his/her work. Use the checklist below.

- ◯ number of slides
- ◯ title, introduction, information, and conclusion
- ◯ number of words in each slide
- ◯ images
- ◯ icons

YOUR DIGITAL PORTFOLIO

Edit your presentation. Then publish it. Upload it to the class portfolio for everyone to see!

REVIEW
UNITS 5 AND 6

VOCABULARY

1 Match the beginnings of the sentences (1–4) with the endings (a–d).

1 I get up at — c
2 I have dinner at a
3 I take a shower
4 I do my

a restaurant on Sundays.
b homework in the afternoon.
c 9 a.m. on weekends.
d in the evening.

2 Complete the sentences with the words below.

• ~~video games~~ • friends • movies • music

1 Susanna plays *video games* with her friends. Her favorite is Super Mario.
2 Arthur and Dylan watch .... on weekends.
3 Lola listens to .... in the evening.
4 I like to hang out with my .... on Saturdays.

3 Look at the images and circle the correct words.

1 I like *PE* / *math*.

2 I hate *science* / *music*.

3 I don't like *math* / *art*.

4 I love *science* / *history*!

4 Read the questions and write the answers. Where do you go to ...

1 clean your hands? *restroom*
2 have lunch? ....
3 talk to a teacher? ....
4 read a book? ....

5 Write affirmative (+) and negative (-) sentences.

1 We / do / homework / on weekdays / (-)
We don't do homework on weekdays.
2 They / have dinner / at home / on Fridays / (+)
....
3 Debbie / take / a shower / in the evening / (+)
....
4 Edmond / play / soccer / at school / (-)
....

6 Write questions and short answers.

1 you / take the bus to school / (+)
Do you take the bus to school?
Yes, I do.
2 your friend / have lunch at home / (+)
....
....
3 your parents / help at the animal center / (+)
....
....
4 your teacher / play the guitar / (-)
....
....

LANGUAGE IN CONTEXT

7 **Write questions for the underlined words in the answers.**

1 *Where do you have lunch with your parents?*
I have lunch with my parents at home.

2 ....
She gets up at 7 a.m.

3 ....
They play volleyball with their friends on weekends.

4 ....
I listen to music in the evening.

8 **Complete Jason's routine with the verbs below.**

• ~~get up~~ • watch • have (3x) • not take • take (2x) • play • not do

Hi! I'm Dale, and this is my friend, Jason. He's a student. He [1] *gets up* at 6 a.m. and he [2] .... breakfast with his family. He [3] .... the train to school – he [4] .... the bus. He [5] .... lunch at school. Then he [6] .... soccer in the afternoon. He goes home at 5 p.m., but he [7] .... his homework. He [8] .... TV! He [9] .... dinner, [10] .... a shower, and then he goes to bed.

9 **Write about your weekend. Use the phrases below and the affirmative and negative forms of the verbs.**

- get up
- hang out with friends
- have breakfast / lunch / dinner
- go to the park / museum
- do homework
- go to bed

CHECK YOUR PROGRESS

I CAN...

- **talk about routines and free-time activities.** 🙂 ○ 🙁 ○
- **use the simple present to discuss routines and free-time activities.** 🙂 ○ 🙁 ○
- **talk about school subjects and places at school.** 🙂 ○ 🙁 ○
- **use the simple present in third person to describe activities at school.** 🙂 ○ 🙁 ○

LEARN TO LEARN

My glossary

Write an example sentence with new words.

breakfast = I have breakfast with my family.

Draw a picture too!

breakfast =

7 WHAT'S HE WEARING?

UNIT GOALS

- Talk about clothes.
- Read a chat between two friends.
- Listen to a friend describing his sister.
- Learn about the Bedouins.
- Talk about an image of someone's clothes.

THINK!

1 "You are what you wear." Do you agree?

2 What do your clothes say about you?

VIDEO 7.1

1 How are Tokyo and London similar?

2 What two things does the video talk about that affect our clothing choices?

VOCABULARY IN CONTEXT

1 7.01 **Match the images with the words below. Then listen, check, and repeat.**

• jacket • pants • shoes • shorts • ~~sweatshirt~~ • T-shirt

www.teenfashion.com

online webstore | log in

FIND A STORE | GIFT CARD | SEARCH

CLOTHES

1

a big red *sweatshirt*

2

blue **jeans**

3

a black ....

4

green ....

5

white ....

6

white **sneakers**

7

a red and blue **shirt**

8

a blue ....

9

black ....

2 **Which clothes in the photos in Exercise 1 do you like? Tell your partner.**

> ♥ I like the jeans!

> ♥♥♥ I love the …!

> I hate the …

3 **Circle the odd one out.**

1 jeans / pants / sweatshirt
2 T-shirt / sneakers / shirt
3 shorts / jacket / sweatshirt
4 jacket / pants / shorts
5 shoes / sneakers / shirt

4 **Make your own picture dictionary for five of the clothes words in Exercise 1.**

USE IT!

5 **Write the names of clothes you wear in the chart. Then tell your partner.**

Clothes I Wear at School	Clothes I Wear on Weekends
I wear shoes at school.	I wear sneakers on weekends.

6 **What are your favorite clothes? Tell your partner.**

> My favorite clothes are my sneakers and sweatshirt.

READING

1 **Look at the page and answer the questions. Check (✓) the correct answers.**

1 **What type of text is it?**
- ◯ a cell phone dialogue between two friends
- ◯ an online blog post

2 **What is the relationship between the two people?**
- ◯ They're brothers.
- ◯ They're friends.

2 🔊 7.02 **Read and listen to the text and check your answers to Exercise 1.**

Hey, Jordan. What's up?

Hi, Nick! I'm at the mall with my dad and my sister. My dad is getting a shirt for work and a sweatshirt for the weekend. My sister is getting a sweatshirt, too. They're buying the same one! I'm buying a new pair of jeans and a new T-shirt 👕 for Jackson's party.

Why? You have lots of T-shirts!! 👕👕👕👕👕 🤔

You're right. I'm not buying it! I'm in the store, but it's closing now. Where are you?

I'm at home. I'm looking at my clothes for the party. I like the brown pants. But I'm not wearing my favorite white T-shirt.

Why not? Wait, what about a black T-shirt?

I don't have one. 😔

I have one. Wear it to the party!

👍👍👍 Cool! Thanks, Jordan! I'm wearing my black jacket and my sneakers.

I'm not wearing my sneakers. I'm wearing my blue shoes. Come to my house after soccer club to go to the party. 👍👍

3 **Look at the emojis in the text. Draw the emoji for each adjective.**

1 happy 😊 2 sad ______ 3 good ______ 4 think ______

4 **Read the text again. Then complete the text below with the correct words.**

Jordan is at the mall with his [1] ___dad___ and his sister. Nick is at [2] __________. They're talking about [3] __________ party. Jordan is in a [4] __________, but he doesn't buy a [5] __________ because he has lots of them. Nick is wearing brown [6] __________, Jordan's [7] __________ T-shirt, and a jacket to the party. Jordan isn't wearing [8] __________.

THINK!

Is it important to look good? Why / Why not?

WORKBOOK p.139

LANGUAGE IN CONTEXT

1 **Look at the examples in the chart. Complete the sentences from Nick and Jordan's chat.**

Present Progressive	
Affirmative (+)	**Negative (-)**
I'**m looking** at my clothes.	I'**m not looking** at my clothes.
You'**re wearing** your blue shoes. We'**re buying** pants. They ...'re buying... the same one.	You'**re not wearing** your sneakers. We'**re not buying** pants. They'**re not buying** the same one.
He'**s** .... a shirt. She'**s** .... a sweatshirt. It .... now.	He'**s not getting** a shirt. She'**s not getting** a sweatshirt. It'**s not closing** now

LOOK!
Use **wear** with clothes.
I'**m wearing** black shoes.
She'**s wearing** new pants.

2 **Use the words to write sentences.**

1 Gina / blue jacket (✓)
Gina is wearing a blue jacket .
She's ...not wearing... a red jacket.

2 Mark / blue shorts (✓)
....
He's .... black shorts.

3 Ingrid / red T-shirt (**X**)
....
She's .... red shirt.

4 Jacob / blue jeans (**X**)
....
He's .... white jeans.

5 Anna / white sneakers (✓)
....
She's .... black shoes.

3 **Nick and Jordan are at Jackson's party. What are they wearing? Write sentences.**

Nick ....
....
Jordan ....
....

USE IT!

I'm wearing blue pants, a green T-shirt …

4 **Work in pairs. You're at a party with Nick and Jordan. Describe what you are wearing.**

WORKBOOK p.136 and p.138 PRACTICE EXTRA

LISTENING AND VOCABULARY

1 **Match the sentences (1–6) with the images (A–F).**

1 She's wearing a hat and glasses.
2 She's wearing a skirt and socks.
3 She's wearing a dress and glasses.
4 She's wearing glasses, a hat, jeans, and a top.
5 She's wearing a jacket, jeans, and a hat.
6 She's wearing black boots, a coat, and a black hat.

2 7.03 **Put the letters in the correct order to make clothes words. Then listen, check, and repeat.**

1 pot .... top ....
2 tosbo ....
3 dsser ....
4 skcso ....
5 atco ....
6 ath ....
7 riskt ....
8 segssla ....

3 7.04 **Look at the images in Exercise 1 and listen to the dialogue. Who is Sergio's sister? Complete the sentence.**

Sergio's sister is the girl in picture ....

4 7.04 **Listen to the dialogue again and circle the correct answers.**

1 Carlos is *waiting* / *not waiting* for Sergio by the movie theater.
2 Sergio's sister is *wearing* / *not wearing* a hat.
3 Carlos is *wearing* / *not wearing* glasses.
4 Carlos is *wearing* / *not wearing* a coat.
5 Sergio's sister is *waiting* / *not waiting* for Sergio by the cafeteria.

WORKBOOK p.136 and p.137

LANGUAGE IN CONTEXT

1 **Complete the questions and answers from the dialogue in the chart. Use the words below.**

- 'm
- are (2x)
- Is
- waiting
- wearing (3x)

Present Progressive		
***Yes/No* Questions**	**Short Answers**	
Am I meeting at the movie theater?	Yes, **I am**.	No, I 'm **not**.
______ you ______ your glasses? **Are** we **waiting** by the library? **Are** they **meeting** in the cafeteria?	Yes, you **are**. Yes, we **are**. Yes, they **are**.	No, you'**re not**. No, we'**re not**. No, they'**re not**.
Is he **wearing** jeans? ______ she ______ for me in the cafeteria? **Is** it **opening** now?	Yes, he **is**. Yes, she **is**. Yes, it **is**.	No, he'**s not**. No, she'**s not**. No, it'**s not**.
***Wh-* Questions**		
What ______ you ______?	I'm ______ my jeans, a green top and green socks.	

2 **Write questions and answers with the words below.**

1 They / play volleyball (**X**) / listen to music (✓)
Are they playing volleyball?
No, they're not. They're listening to music.

2 Julie / go to bed (**X**) / do her homework (✓)
______
______

3 Tom and his dad / play soccer (**X**) / play video games (✓)
______
______

4 Carlos / buy jeans (**X**) / look at T-shirts (✓)
______
______

5 Emma, Jo, and Liz / have dinner (**X**) / have lunch (✓)
______
______

LOOK!
They'**re meeting** in the cafeteria **now** / **right now** / **at this moment**.
(at the time of speaking)

3 **Write questions and answer them for you.**

1 What / wear? ______
______

2 What / your teacher / do? ______
______

3 What / your best friend / do / now? ______
______

USE IT!

4 **Work in pairs. Ask and answer the questions in Exercise 3. Then compare your answers.**

WORKBOOK p.136 and p.138 PRACTICE EXTRA

AROUND THE WORLD

HOW TO DRESS IN THE DESERT

Every month we have a new article about clothes and culture. This month we're talking to Ahmad Mostafa.

My name is Ahmad Mostafa abu-Rabia Sulaym, and I'm a 13-year-old Bedouin from the Arabian desert. I'm an artist, and I'm sending two of my pictures. They show the type of clothes that we wear in our community.

In this picture, my brother Abdulah is next to one of our camels. But wait ... Is Abdulah wearing a dress? Yes, he is, because it's very hot in the desert so we wear loose clothes. We all wear dresses: women, girls, boys, and men. He's not wearing a hat on his head, but a *ghutra*. This protects his head from the sun. He's wearing sandals, too, because the sand is really hot.

And what are the people doing in this picture? It's the end of the day, and the men are sitting and listening to traditional stories. Some are wearing coats, or *furwahs*, because the nights are cold. Who is the woman wearing a black dress? And what is she doing? Well, that's my aunt Aisha, and she's working. She's bringing water to the camp.

1 **Look at the article, the titles, and the images. Then answer the question. Check (✓) the correct answer.**

What do you think the article is about?

- ◯ families and traditions in the desert
- ◯ water in the desert
- ◯ people's clothes in the desert

2 **Read the article quickly. Check (✓) the words in the article.**

◯ dress ◯ glasses ◯ pants ◯ jacket ◯ coat ◯ clothes

3 🔈 7.05 **Read and listen to the article. Check your answers to Exercises 1 and 2.**

4 **Match the beginnings of the sentences (1–4) with the endings (a–d).**

1	Ahmad	a	is working.
2	Abdulah	b	is sending his pictures to the magazine.
3	The men	c	are sitting and listening to stories.
4	Aisha	d	is wearing a dress and a *ghutra*.

5 **Read the article again. Write *T* (true) or *F* (false) next to the statements.**

1 Abdulah is an artist. F
2 In the desert, women wear dresses and men wear pants. ....
3 Hats are common to protect from the desert sun. ....
4 Sandals protect your feet from the hot sand. ....
5 Nights are always hot in the desert. ....
6 Bedouin women are responsible for getting water. ....

WORDS IN CONTEXT

6 **Complete the sentences with the words below.**

• cold • hot • sandals • loose • sand

1 People wear coats to protect them from .... temperatures.
2 The Bedouins usually wear .... clothes, because it's hot in the desert.
3 People wear .... in the summer, not shoes or sneakers.
4 The .... in the desert is very hot and it's difficult to walk there.
5 People don't wear coats when it's ....

WEBQUEST

Learn more! Check (✓) *True* or *False*.
The Bedouin people live in the desert for some months every year.

◯ **True** ◯ **False**

THINK!

1 **What clothes do people in your country wear?**

2 **Do clothes reflect our personality and culture?**

VIDEO

7.2

1 **Which places can you see in the video?**

2 **What are your favorite clothes in the video?**

SPEAKING

GIVING OPINIONS

1 7.06 **Read and listen to two friends talking about clothes. Where are they?**

Lucca Hi, Georgia. Are you wearing a new **sweatshirt**?
Georgia Yeah. It's my **brother's**. Do you like it?
Lucca Um … not really. I prefer your **red sweatshirt**.
Georgia Well, that's my favorite. But this **sweatshirt** is **nice**.
Lucca Hmmm, I guess it's a bit **big**.
Georgia Really?
Lucca Yes, and I think it's **really old**.
Georgia You're right!
Lucca What are you doing?
Georgia I'm changing my **sweatshirt**!

LIVING ENGLISH

2 **Complete the mini dialogues with the expressions below.**

- I prefer
- Not really
- I guess

1
A Do you like my new sneakers?
B No, ________________ your old ones.

2
A Where's my new sweater?
B I don't know. In the closet, ________________.

3
A Do you like my pants?
B ________________ – sorry. I don't like green pants.

3 7.07 **Listen and repeat the expressions.**

PRONUNCIATION

4 7.08 **Listen and repeat.**

This is my brother's sweatshirt.

You're right.

5 7.06 **Listen to the dialogue again. Then practice with a partner.**

6 **Role play a new dialogue. Follow the steps.**

1 **Take a picture of your friend in nice clothes.**
2 **Change the words in blue to write a new dialogue in your notebook.**
3 **Practice your dialogue with a partner.**
4 **Present your dialogue to the class.**

YOUR DIGITAL PORTFOLIO

Record your dialogue. Then upload it to your class digital portfolio.

PRACTICE EXTRA

8 GET MOVING!

UNIT GOALS

- Talk about sports.
- Read about people and sports.
- Listen to a podcast.
- Learn about why we do sports.
- Write an email.

THINK!

1 What sports do you like?
2 Why is it important to do sports?

VIDEO 8.1

1 Who can do sports?
2 Say two things that sport can teach us.

VOCABULARY IN CONTEXT

1 8.01 **Choose the correct verbs to complete the advertisement. Then listen and check your answers.**

Sports

1 ***Swim / dance*** in the ocean with your friends.

Come to Andalusia, Spain to do sports!

2 ***Ice-skate / Play volleyball*** or ***run / surf*** on the beach.

3 ***Swim / ski*** in the mountains!

5 And in the evening, ***dance / ski*** to great music with your friends!

4 ***Ice-skate / play volleyball*** at the ice rink.

2 8.02 **Listen and number the words in the order you hear them from 1–7. Then listen again, check, and repeat.**

.... swim	.... ski
.... surf	.... ice-skate
.... play volleyball	.... dance
...1... run	

3 Organize the verbs below in the circles. Do you use your hand or foot?

- ~~kick~~
- throw
- catch
- walk
- run

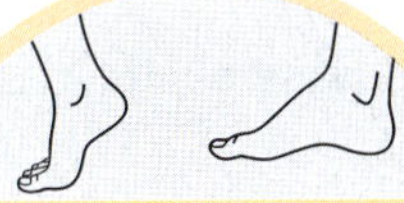

kick

4 8.03 Match the images with the words in Exercise 3. Then listen, check, and repeat.

1

2

3

4

5

USE IT!

5 What sports do you do? Mark (✓) or (X).

	Me	My Partner
ski	○	○
run	○	○
dance	○	○
play basketball	○	○
surf	○	○
ice-skate	○	○
swim	○	○

6 Work in pairs. Ask and answer the questions. Mark (✓) or (X) for your partner.

What sports do you do?

I dance, I run, and I swim.
I don't surf or ski.

WORKBOOK p.141 PRACTICE EXTRA

READING

1 **Look at the text and the images. Then check (✓) the correct answer and answer the question.**

1 **What type of text is this?**

◯ a blog about athletes ◯ a pamphlet with recommendations

2 **Who is your favorite athlete? Why?**

....

www.sportschamps.com

Theo Curin is from France. He swims in the Paralympics. He swims for four hours a day, and on weekends, he swims in competitions. He can swim very fast, but he can't ski or ice-skate.

Saki Kumagai is a Japanese soccer player, but she plays for a French team. She loves soccer, but she likes other sports too, like basketball and volleyball. She can kick the ball very hard, but she can't swim very well.

Clarence Munyai is from South Africa. He lives with his mom and dad, his three sisters, and his brother. He can run very fast! He can run 200 meters in 20 seconds! He can play soccer, but he can't dance.

3 comments

Max

Max I love Saki! She's awesome. I can kick a ball very hard, but I can't play volleyball.

reply

Julia

Wow! Théo is my hero. I can swim 100 meters in three minutes, but I can't swim fast like Théo!

reply

Helena

I run every day for two hours. I can run fast, but Clarence is great! He can run 100 meters in about 10 seconds. I can't! 😔

reply

2 8.04 **Read and listen to the text. Check (✓) the correct person in the chart.**

	Theo	Saki	Clarence
kick the ball very hard	◯	◯	◯
run very fast	◯	◯	◯
swim very well	◯	◯	◯
swim very fast	◯	◯	◯
play basketball	◯	◯	◯
play soccer	◯	◯	◯

3 **Read the text again and answer the questions.**

1 What does Theo do?

Theo swims.

2 Where is Saki from?

....

3 What are Saki's favorite sports?

....

4 Who does Clarence live with?

....

5 Does Clarence play soccer?

....

6 Who can swim 100 meters in 180 seconds?

....

THINK!

Are sports important? Why / Why not?

WORKBOOK p.143

LANGUAGE IN CONTEXT

1 **Look at the examples in the chart. Complete the sentences from the blog.**

***Can*: Ability**	
Affirmative (+)	**Negative (-)**
I ___can___ run fast.	I **can't** run fast.
He ______ play soccer. She ______ kick the ball. It **can** dance.	He ______ dance. She ______ swim. It **can't** dance.
We **can** dance. You **can** ski. They **can** play volleyball.	We **can't** dance. You **can't** ski. They **can't** play volleyball.

LOOK!
can't = cannot
I **can't** play volleyball.
I **cannot** play volleyball.

2 **Complete the sentences with *can* or *can't* and the verbs in parentheses.**

1 I ___can play___ (play ✓) volleyball.
2 He ______ (walk **X**) to school.
3 She ______ (surf ✓) in the ocean.
4 They ______ (eat **X**) pizza.
5 You ______ (dance ✓) very well.
6 We ______ (ice-skate **X**) today.

***Yes/No* Questions**	**Short Answers**
Can I/you/he/she/it/we/they dance?	**Yes**, I/you/he/she/it/we/they **can**.
	No, I/you/he/she/it/we/they **can't**.

3 **Write questions and answers about what Marta and Luis *can* and *can't* do.**

	play volleyball	run fast	dance
1 Marta	X	✓	✓
2 Luis	✓	✓	X

1 ___Can___ Marta ___play volleyball? No, she can't.___
___Can___ Luis ___play volleyball? Yes, he can.___
2 ______ Marta and Luis ______
3 ______ Marta ______
______ Luis ______

USE IT!

4 **Write questions for your partner with *can* and the words below.**

• dance • run fast • ice-skate • spell your name • play soccer • swim

___Can you dance?___

5 **Ask and answer the questions with your partner.**

Can you dance?
No, I can't.

WORKBOOK p.140 and p.142 PRACTICE EXTRA

LISTENING AND VOCABULARY

1 **Look at the image and check (✓) the correct answer. What does it represent?**

◯ an infographic　　◯ an interview

2 **8.05 Look at the image. Complete the sentences with the words below. Then listen to the podcast and check.**

- ~~do exercise~~
- don't eat junk food
- don't go to bed late
- don't sit down all day
- drink water
- eat healthy food

3 **Complete the chart with expressions that have similar meanings. Use the infographic to help you.**

Do exercise.	1 Don't sit down all day.
2	Don't eat junk food.
Go to bed early.	3 ....
4	Don't drink soda.

4 **8.06 Listen, check, and repeat.**

5 **8.07 Listen to Maria and Sergio. Check (✓) what they do.**

	Maria	Sergio
play basketball	✓	◯
eat junk food	◯	◯
eat healthy food	◯	◯
play on the cell phone	◯	◯
do exercise	◯	◯

WORKBOOK p.140 and p.141

LANGUAGE IN CONTEXT

1 Complete the instructions from the podcast in the chart. Use the words below.

• ~~Put~~ • Don't eat • Go • Come • Don't take

Imperatives	
Affirmative (+)	**Negative (-)**
___Put___ on your sneakers.	________ the bus to school.
________ to the park.	________ junk food.
________ on!	**Don't drink** soda!

2 Match the beginnings of the sentences (1–6) with the endings (a–f).

1 Don't write
2 Don't forget
3 Eat
4 Do
5 Get up
6 Don't use

a your homework every day.
b to drink two liters of water every day.
c your cell phone in class.
d on the wall!
e now. It's ten o'clock!
f fruit to be healthy!

3 Look at the images. Write affirmative and negative imperative sentences.

• eat • go to bed late • run • watch TV • wear my T-shirt

1

2

5

3

4

USE IT!

4 Work in pairs. Give instructions and act them out.

Catch a ball!

Drink water!

WORKBOOK p.140 and p.142 PRACTICE EXTRA

ACROSS THE CURRICULUM

PHYSICAL EDUCATION

Different Sports for Different Benefits

SPORTSACTIVE.ORG

Children play sports because they can have fun with their friends, they feel good playing, and they like to compete.

But for **scientists**, sports are really good for you

physically,

emotionally,

mentally,

and socially.

Scientists say sports can ...

- increase muscle strength and flexibility.
- reduce stress, depression, and obesity.
- improve concentration, memory, and school work.
- teach collaboration and respect.

Scientists also say that it's good to practice different types of sports, not only one. Why?

When you play different sports that have a variety of movements and skills, you don't feel demotivated. Different sports develop different physical abilities.

Sports like running, soccer, and swimming develop your cardio activity and respiratory capacity.

Yoga and Pilates are excellent for flexibility.

And activities like weight training can make you strong.

So, to be healthy and strong, add **60 minutes** of sports to your day, and go for it: you can try different types of sports, practice every day, and enjoy life!

1 **Read the text quickly and check (✓) the correct answer.**

1 **The objective of the text is ...**
◯ to ask children to take part in physical education classes.
◯ to inform about multiple benefits of sports.
◯ to tell a story with attractive images and lettering.

2 **You can say that the text is ...**
◯ artistic. ◯ critical. ◯ educational.

2 8.08 **Read and listen to the text. Check (✓) the true sentences.**

◯ All children play sports.
◯ All sports develop the same physical skills.
◯ It's a good idea to practice different sports.
◯ Scientists do lots of sports.
◯ Sports are fun.

3 **What are the activities below good for? Read the text again and complete the chart.**

• ~~running~~ • Pilates • soccer • swimming • weight training • yoga

Cardio Activity	Flexibility	Strength
running.		

4 **Match the beginnings of the sentences (1–5) with the endings (a–e).**

1 Different sports can develop different — b
2 To be flexible,
3 Practice sports for 60 minutes a day
4 Scientists say that sports are good for you
5 Sports can teach

a collaboration and respect.
b physical abilities.
c do yoga and Pilates.
d physically, mentally, and socially.
e to be healthy and strong.

WORDS IN CONTEXT

5 **Find in the text ...**

1 the opposite of "reduce": ____________
2 a synonym for "abilities": ____________
3 a word for "to make something better":
____

6 **Complete the sentences with the words below.**

• develop • strength • strong
• weight training

1 ____________ makes your muscles big.
2 Exercise makes you healthy and ____________.
3 Damien does different sports. He wants to ____________ new physical skills.
4 Djamila has the ____________ to win a gold medal at the Olympics.

WEBQUEST

Learn more! Make a list of other sports that ...
1 create big muscles.
2 increase flexibility.
3 help cardio activity.

THINK!

1 **Do you think these types of texts are effective to motivate people? Why / Why not?**
2 **What can you do to have 60 minutes of sports practice every day?**

VIDEO

8.2

1 **How many sports can you remember from the video?**
2 **Where is the mermaid swimming?**

WRITING

From: samhans@youmail.com
To: pesmith@youmail.com
Subject: PE classes ①

② Dear Mr. Smith,

③ I'm Sam and I'm writing to you to suggest a new activity for our PE class. My favorite sport is basketball. This is a good activity for our PE class because we can become strong, develop our muscles, and work with coordination. Basketball is an activity that we can do in the gymnasium. It's a good activity because we can improve teamwork and have fun.

④ Best wishes,
Sam

1 🔊 8.09 **Read and listen to the email and answer the questions.**

1 **Who is writing the email?** ....

2 **Who is receiving the email?** ....

2 **What's the main idea in the email?**

◯ to propose basketball as a PE activity
◯ to express all the students' opinions
◯ to show how PE classes can be fun

3 **Number the parts of the email from 1–4.**

.... greeting
.... introduction
.... closing
.... subject

4 **Read the *Look!* box. Underline examples of *because* in the email.**

5 **Plan an email, giving your suggestion for a new activity in PE classes.**

1 **Think about the activities you like.**
2 **Use Sam's email as a model to plan your text.**
3 **Write the first version of your email. Make sure you include the parts of an email in Exercise 3.**

LOOK!
Use **because** to give a reason why.
I'm writing to you **because** ...

6 **Switch presentations with a partner and check his/her work. Use the checklist below.**

◯ name of person sending the email
◯ name of person receiving the email
◯ greeting
◯ introduction and suggestion for a new activity
◯ subject
◯ closing

YOUR DIGITAL PORTFOLIO
Edit your email. Then publish it. Upload it to the class portfolio for everyone to see!

REVIEW
UNITS 7 AND 8

VOCABULARY

1 **Match the sentences (1–4) with the images (A–D).**

A  ○

B  ○

C  ○

D  ○

1 This is my favorite coat. It's nice!
2 I'm wearing a red shirt. I love it!
3 I like informal clothes. This sweatshirt is cool.
4 I'm wearing my new pants. They're great.

2 **Look at the images. What do you wear in the situations below?**

1 

2 

3 

----

3 **Circle the odd one out.**

1 surf / swim / (dance)
2 run / iceskate / ski
3 volleyball / surf / soccer
4 top / boots / socks

4 **Complete the sentences.**

1 Don't drink ______ soda.
2 ______ to bed late.
3 ______ exercise.
4 ______ junk food.

5 **Rewrite the sentences. Use the information in parentheses.**

1 I'm wearing a T-shirt. (- / shirt)
I'm not wearing a T-shirt. I'm wearing a shirt.
2 She's not wearing boots. (+)
______
3 They're wearing shorts. (- / jeans)
______
4 We're not wearing white T-shirts. (+)
______

LANGUAGE IN CONTEXT

6 Circle the correct answers.

1 Are you and Greg meeting in the cafeteria?
   a Yes, they are. ~~~~ (b) No, we're not.
2 What are you wearing?
   a I'm wearing jeans. b I'm at the library.
3 Are they wearing their glasses?
   a Yes, they are. b No, we're not.
4 Are you listening to music?
   a No, I'm doing homework. b Yes, I'm playing video games.

7 Read the chart and write sentences about what the people *can* and *can't* do.

	kick a ball	catch a ball	play soccer	throw a ball
Amina	✓	X	✓	
Dylan		✓	X	
Bella	✓	X		✓
Xavier	X	✓		X

1 *Amina can kick a ball and play soccer, but she can't catch a ball.*
2 ....
3 ....
4 ....

8 Write questions. Then answer the questions so they are true for you.

1 play soccer
   Can you play soccer? No, I can't.
2 throw a ball
   ....
3 ice-skate
   ....
4 dance
   ....

9 Look at the pictures and write sentences.

1 

Drink water.

2 

....

3 

....

4 

....

CHECK YOUR PROGRESS

I CAN…

- talk about clothes. 🙂 ○ 🙁 ○
- use the present progressive to describe clothes. 🙂 ○ 🙁 ○
- talk about sports and skills. 🙂 ○ 🙁 ○
- use *can* and imperatives to say what people can do. 🙂 ○ 🙁 ○

LEARN TO LEARN

Vocabulary Categorization

You can categorize groups of words with other words, for example, *kick*, *throw*, *catch*, *walk*, and *run*. Use them with the nouns *hand* and *foot* to help you remember them.

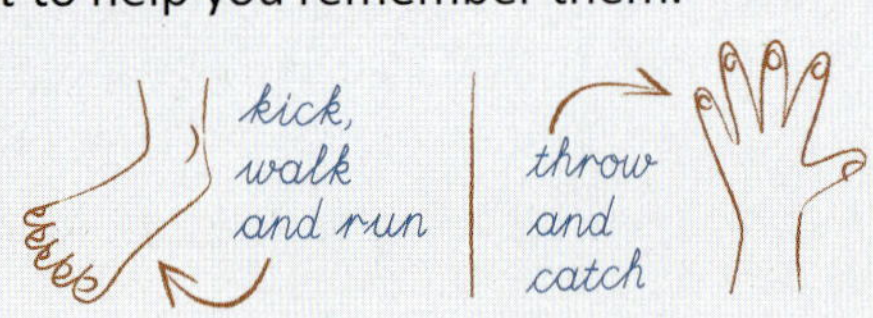

GLOBAL CHANGER EXTRAS

READING 1

ACROSS THE CURRICULUM / MATH

A CLASS SURVEY

1 Look at the charts and circle the correct words.

1 The information in the charts is in *images / paragraphs*.
2 The information is about *teachers / students*.

2 Analyze the charts. Then answer the questions for you.

1 What is your favorite thing? ....
2 What is your favorite place? ....
3 What is your favorite activity? ....

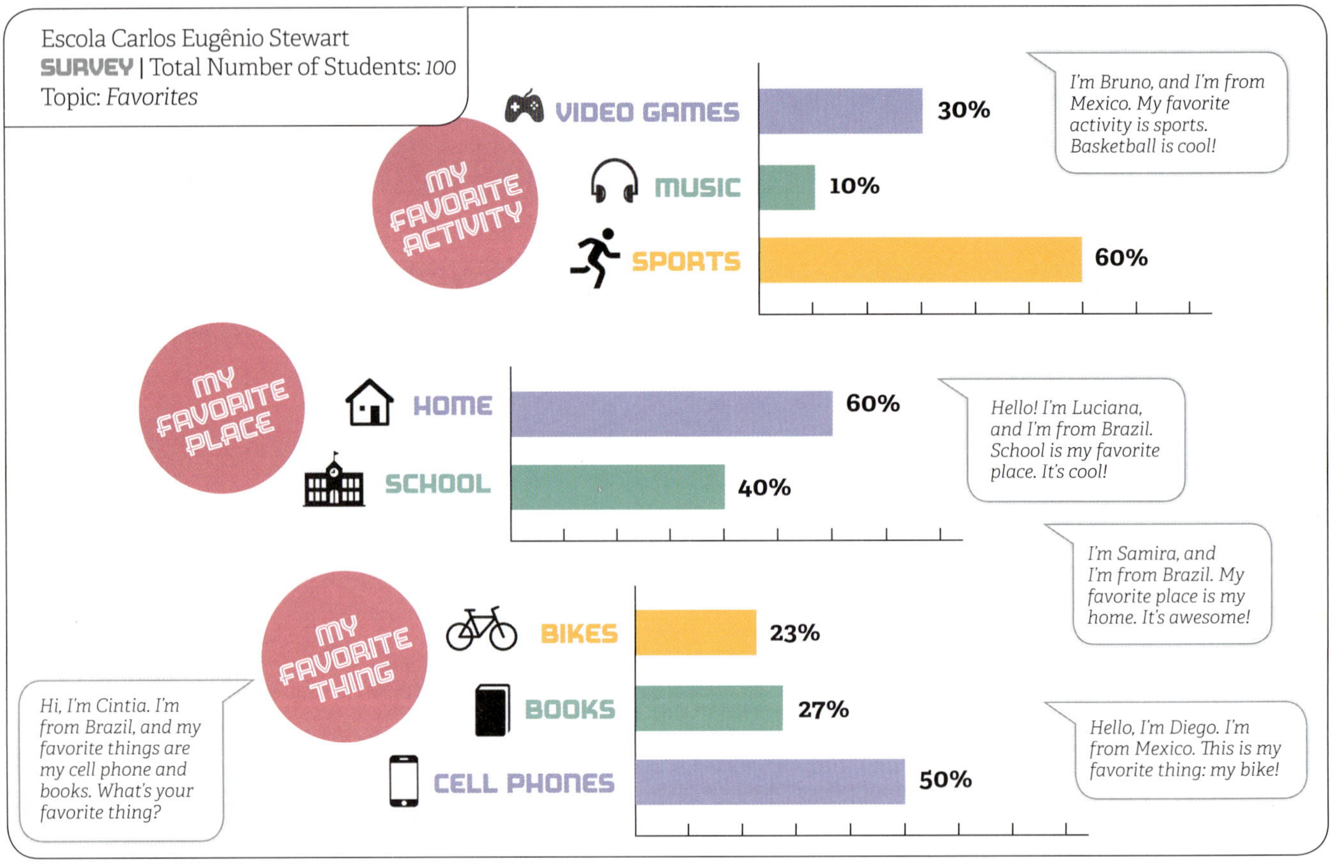

3 R.01 Read and listen to the survey. Circle the correct answers.

1 The cell phone is the favorite thing for … of the students.
a 17% b 21% c 50%

2 School is the favorite place for … of the students.
a 40% b 50% c 60%

3 Music is the favorite activity for … % of the students.
a 10 b 30 c 60

4 … is the favorite activity for 30% of the students.
a Music b Sports c Video games

THINK!

Look at your answers in Exercise 2. Are your results similar to the graphs?

READING 2

AROUND THE WORLD

UNUSUAL HOMES

1 R.02 **Read and listen to the text. Check (✓) the correct answer.**

What is the objective of the author?

◯ to talk about his home ◯ to talk about a different type of hotel ◯ to talk about types of homes

My Home is a Cave

Where is your home? My home is a cave! There are beautiful cave homes around the world. Look!

Look at this hotel in the Cederberg Mountains in South Africa, 240 km from Cape Town. The cave is old, but the windows are very modern!

These cave homes in Matmata, Tunisia, are very old. There are about 2,000 people in this community and the caves are perfect for families!

The Stadsaal caves in South Africa are not homes, but there are paintings here! There are some very old paintings of elephants on the walls. The paintings are over 1,000 years old.

What part of the home is this?

Correct! It's the kitchen! Cool, isn't it? There are no windows, but there are plates on the walls.

These homes are great!
What's your favorite cave home?

2 **Circle the correct words.**

1 Cave homes (*are*) / *are not* beautiful.
2 The cave home in South Africa *is* / *is not* a hotel.
3 The caves in Stadsaal *are* / *are not* homes.
4 The cave homes in Tunisia *are* / *are not* new.
5 There *are* / *are not any* windows in the kitchen in the cave home in Tunisia.

3 **Match the beginnings of the sentences (1–5) with the endings (a–e).**

1 The cave homes in Tunisia are old, ——	a in the Cederberg Mountains.
2 There are plates on the walls	b but they're perfect for families.
3 There's an old cave	c but the windows are very modern.
4 The hotel in South Africa is old,	d in the caves in South Africa.
5 There are old paintings	e in the kitchen in the cave in Tunisia.

THINK!

Are cave homes awesome? Why / Why not?

READING 3

ACROSS THE CURRICULUM / GEOGRAPHY

WATER

1 Complete the sentence.

I use water for ....

2 R.03 Read and listen to the text. Are your ideas from Exercise 1 in the text?

Water: An Important Resource

February

Hi there! I'm Aimee, and I'm 13 years old. I live in Nyakabingo. It's a small place in Africa. There isn't clean water in Nyakabingo, and it is a big problem for my family and friends. My mom, my brothers, and I walk for three hours to get water. We take a container. With the water in the container, it's about 45 kilos – the same as a baby hippo!

October

But now things are different! There's clean water in my school. Now there's a garden with fresh vegetables and fruit. We eat them at lunchtime! The water is safe and the bathrooms and kitchen are clean. My family and friends go to school to get clean water. Now we don't walk for hours! I have time to study and have an education. My mom and dad work in the community and we all feel great!

Is there clean water in your home and in your school? Many people in the world don't have clean water, so remember, water is very important – let's preserve it.

3 Read the text again and complete the sentences with the words below.

• ~~difficult~~ • container • clean • fresh • safe • hippo

1 It's ....difficult.... to get clean water in Nyakabingo.
2 Aimee and her family use a .... to carry water.
3 A baby .... is about 45 kilos!
4 The vegetables and fruit at Aimee's school are ....
5 The water in Aimee's school is ....
6 The bathrooms and the kitchen in the school are ....

4 Check (✓) the correct sentences.

1 Aimee is 13 years old. ✓
2 There's clean water in Aimee's village now. ○
3 There isn't a yard at Aimee's school. ○
4 Aimee has time to study now. ○
5 There's clean water for everybody in the world. ○

THINK!

Where is your water from? What do you do to preserve water?

READING 4

AROUND THE WORLD

MY INUIT FAMILY

1 **Look at the photo and the text. Who is the author?** ____________________

2 **Where is the text from? Circle the correct words to complete the sentence.**

The text is from *a blog / a book*.

www.inuitareus.com/bios/1283

Home / About Me / Contact Me

About Me Hi, and welcome to my blog! My name's Toklo. I'm 12 years old and I live in Alaska with my family. Look at this photo. There are five people in my family: my dad, my mom, my brother, my grandma, and me. In this photo, I'm wearing a brown coat, brown pants, and boots.

In my family, we don't use animals to make clothes. We buy modern clothes because they're comfortable. But some families make clothes with animal fur and animal skins to keep warm.

Are we Eskimo people? No, we're not. Eskimo is not the correct word. We are Inuit. We live in other places, too, like Canada, Siberia, and Greenland.

It's very cold here. Sometimes it's -40°C. It's impossible to go out without the right clothes. I don't wear regular clothes like T-shirts, sweatshirts, shorts, or sneakers. It's too cold for that! I wear special shirts, pants, and jackets that protect my body. But I have to wear two pairs of boots and two hats!

I hope you enjoy my blog! Please comment on the post – it's great to get to know you!

3 R.04 **Read and listen to the text. Complete the chart with the words in the text.**

Family Members	Clothes	Places
dad	coat	Alaska

4 **Read the text again and complete the sentences with one word.**

1 Toklo is from Alaska.
2 There are ____________ people in Toklo's family.
3 Toklo and his family wear ____________ clothes.
4 Toklo and his family don't wear ____________ clothes because it's very cold.
5 *Inuit* people live in Alaska, Siberia, ____________ and Greenland.

THINK!

1 **What are "special clothes" for you?**
2 **What are "traditional clothes" in your country?**

PUZZLES & GAMES

UNIT 1

1 Find and name four more things.

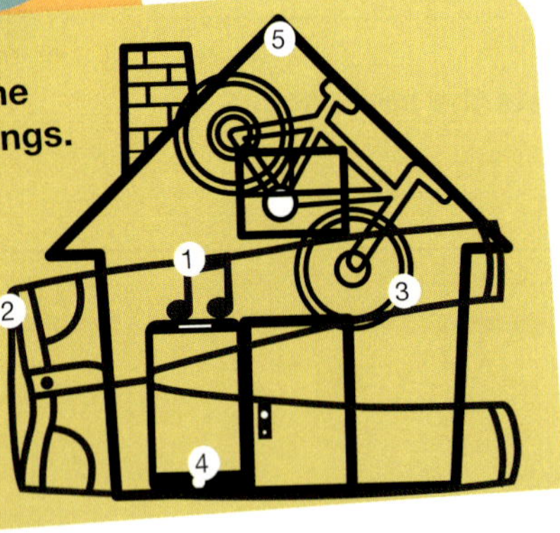

1 music
2 ______
3 ______
4 ______
5 ______

2 Find the words with the same color. Put the words in the correct order to make four questions.

What Who your phone number? are is you? teacher? is is How address? is your old your your What name? What

What is your name?

______

______

______

______

Now answer the questions for you.

UNIT 2

3 Write the words in the chart. Use the numbers to find the secret word.

- American
- Brazilian
- British
- ~~French~~
- Japanese
- Russian
- South African
- Spanish

F R E N C H (12, 1)
_ M _ _ _ _ _ N (7)
_ R _ _ I _ _ (10)
_ _ _ _ _ _ _ E (2)
S _ _ _ _ _ _ (9)
_ U _ _ _ _ _ (13, 4)
_ _ _ _ _ _ _ A _ (11, 8, 6)
S _ _ _ _ _ _ _ _ _ _ _ (5, 3)

Secret Word: _ _ _ _ _ _ _ _ _ _ _ _ _
1 2 3 4 5 6 7 8 9 10 11 12 13

4 Look at the colors in the flags and the names. Complete the questions and answers.

1 Is LUIS Brazilian? Yes, he is.
2 ______ JOSE and DIEGO Mexican?
No, ______ . They're ______ .
3 ______ AMHLE South African?
Yes, she ______ .
4 Are YOU American?
______ , I'm ______ .
I'm ______ .
5 Is JAVIER Spanish?
No ______ . He's ______ .

UNIT 3

1 Where are they? Use the code and write the places.

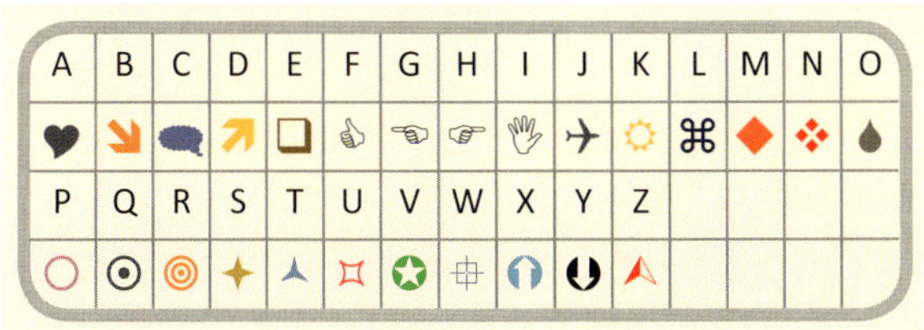

1 Laura is in the ______ *kitchen.*
2 Miguel is in the ______ ______
3 Beatriz is in the ______ ______
4 Lucas is in the ______ ______
5 Enzo is in the ______ ______
6 Camila is in the ______ ______

2 Put the letters in the correct order to complete the questions. Then look at the bedroom and answer.

1 Is there a EBD *bed?*
______
2 Is there a SOLECT ______?
______
3 Are there any RISCHA ______?
______
4 Is there a BALTE ______?
______
5 Are there two WOSNDWI ______?
______

UNIT 4

3 Who am I? Complete the sentences about a family.

- ~~aunt~~
- grandpa
- dad
- grandparents
- grandma
- uncle

1 My cousin's mom is my *aunt.*
2 My dad's brother is my ______
3 My dad's mom is my ______
4 My mom's dad is my ______
5 My parent's parents are my ______
6 My sister's dad is my ______

4 Look at the code, complete the questions with the vowels.

1 D_ y__r gr_ndp_r_nts h_v_ f__r h__r? (o u, a, e, i)
Do your grandparents have fair hair?
2 D_ y__ h_v_ thr__ br_th_rs?
______
3 D__s y__r d_d h_ve _ s_st_r?
______
4 D__s y__r m_m h_ve bl__ _y_s?
______
5 D__s y__r fr__nd h_v_ l_ng h__r?
______

5 Now answer the questions for you.

UNIT 5

1 Complete the crossword.

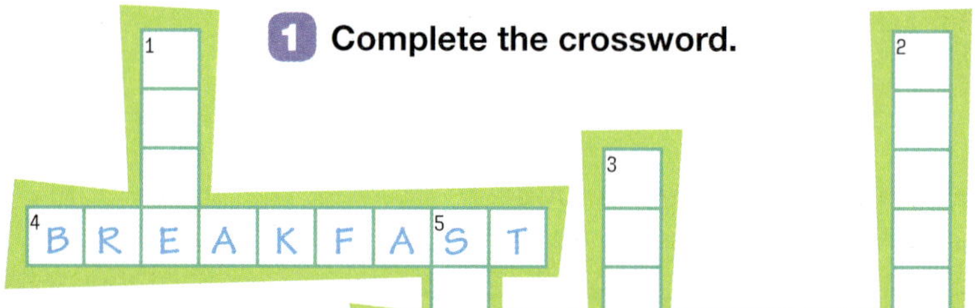

Across

4 HAVE B REAKFAST

6 PLAY V

8 GO TO B

Down

1 GO H

2 GO TO S

3 DO MY H

5 TAKE A S

7 TAKE THE B

2 Look at the images and find the correct sentences.

1 

2 

3 

1 I H A V E D I N N E R W I T H M Y F A M I L Y I D O M Y Ω H O M E W O R K I N T H E A F T E R N O O N I H A V E L U N C H A T H O M E

I do my homework in the afternoon.

2 I G O T O S C H O O L I H A V E B R E A K F A S T I G E T U P A T E I G H T I T A K E T H E B U S T O S C H O O L I G O T O B E D

3 I P L A Y V O L L E Y B A L L I T A K E T H E B U S Y O U T A K E A S H O W E R A T N I G H T Y O U H A V E B R E A K F A S T A T S C H O O L

UNIT 6

3 Find seven places in school.

R	S	C	I	E	N	T	L	I	B	R	C	A	R
E	C	A	F	E	T	E	L	A	B	O	A	L	F
S	C	I	E	N	C	E	L	A	B	E	F	O	I
T	R	E	S	T	R	O	I	C	A	F	E	T	E
R	G	Y	M	N	A	S	B	A	T	H	T	U	L
O	R	O	O	M	R	R	R	B	R	A	E	N	T
O	L	I	B	R	O	A	A	D	I	N	R	G	E
M	T	E	A	C	O	Y	R	I	N	G	I	E	A
S	S	R	E	H	M	S	Y	H	A	L	A	R	C
T	E	A	C	H	E	R	S	L	O	U	N	G	E
A	A	T	H	L	E	T	I	C	F	I	E	L	D
G	Y	M	N	A	S	I	U	M	A	T	H	L	H

4 Put the blocks in order and write the questions.

1 OES | OP | EN? | N D | TH | E LI | RY | BRA | WHE

When does the library open?

2 T D | THE | WHA | ER L | HE D | AB? | O IN | OES S | MAK

3 D | 3-D PR | AK | ER L | OES | AB HA | THE M | INTER? | VE A

4 EY R | EAD | WHE | ITE BOO | KS? | O TH | RE D | THE | IR FAVOR

UNIT 7

1 **Look at the image. Write the clothes you see.**

1 pants
2
3
4
5
6

2 **Look at the images and find four differences. What is different in Picture 2?**

Picture 1

Picture 2

1 In picture 2, Sam and Jess aren't watching a movie. They're having breakfast.

2 Sarah ______

3 Emma ______

4 Max and Bill ______

5 Jill and Liz ______

UNIT 8

3 **Look at the images and complete the sentences.**

1 I  ski in the mountains or  ______ at the ice rink.

2 I  ______ with my friends on the weekends.

3 Do you  ______ and  ______ ?

4 They  ______ with their friends.

4 **Put the phrases in the correct order to make four descriptions.**

- Jose and Fernando are from Spain. They're
- run very fast.
- she can't dance.
- Finn is from Liverpool in the
- they can't swim very fast.
- United Kingdom. He is 12 years old. He can play basketball very
- Sylvie is French. She's from Paris, in
- well, and he can run very fast, too.
- Clara and Caterina are from Mexico. They can ski. Clara can
- France. She can play volleyball and run, but
- 11 years old. They can surf very well, but
- ice-skate, but Caterina can't. Caterina can

Finn is from Liverpool in the United Kingdom. He is 12 years old He can play basketball very well, and he can run very fast, too.

PROJECT
DESCRIBING FAMILIES

MAKE A CLASS POSTER ABOUT YOUR FAMILY.

1 Look at the poster on page 107 and check (✓) the correct answers.

1 Who is the poster for?
 ◯ my class ◯ my family
2 What is the poster about?
 ◯ a family ◯ a famous person's family

2 Read the poster. Complete the family tree with the names of people in Liam's family.

3 Read the poster again and answer the questions.

1 Where is Liam from?

....

2 Where is Liam's mom from?

....

3 Where is Liam's dad from?

....

4 Who is Xavier?

....

5 What is Liam's sister's name?

....

THINK!

1 **Who is important to Liam?**
2 **Who in your family is important to you?**

PROJECT TASK

1 PLAN

1 Choose a person you admire.
2 Find out about his/her family. Find photos or draw a family tree.
3 Write your text. Remember to include personal information about him/her, information about his or her family, and your opinion.
4 Design your poster.
5 Check grammar, spelling, and punctuation.

2 YOUR DIGITAL PORTFOLIO

Upload your poster to the class portfolio for everyone to see! Present your poster to the class.

3 REFLECT

Which is your favorite poster? Why?

Liam Ferreira

Liam Xavier Raul Ferreira is a student and a guitar player. His birthday is on March 9th. He's very tall. He's 1.75 meters tall! He's from Sao Paulo in Brazil.

There are four people in his family: Liam, his mom, his dad, and his sister. His family is very important to him.

His mom's name is **Emily**. She's from England in the United Kingdom. His father's name is **Gabriel** and he's from Brazil. Liam's middle names are Xavier and Raul. They're from his grandpas. His English grandpa's name is Xavier, and Raul is from his family in Brazil.

Liam has a sister. Her name is Sophia. She's a student and a singer. She has many followers on Instagram. Liam and Sophia are brother and sister, and they're also good friends.

Liam is my best friend!

PROJECT
TALKING ABOUT SPORTS

MAKE AN INFOGRAPHIC: A CLASS SURVEY REPORT.

1 Look at the infographic from a school magazine on page 109 and check (✓) the correct answers.

1 **Who is the infographic for?**
- ◯ students at school
- ◯ the school soccer team

2 **What is the infographic about?**
- ◯ favorite sports
- ◯ the sports students do

2 Read the infographic and circle the correct answers.

1 There are … boys in Class 7A.
a 34 **b** 12 **c** 22

2 … girls can dance.
a 9 **b** 12 **c** 13

3 … boys can play basketball.
a 6 **b** 12 **c** 15

4 … girls can swim very fast.
a 6 **b** 8 **c** 12

3 What questions do you ask? Write the questions in the survey.

1 play soccer?
Can you play soccer?

2 run fast?
....

3 dance well?
....

4 play basketball?
....

5 swim very fast?
....

THINK!

1 **Do you do sports with your family? Who?**

2 **Why are sports good for you?**

PROJECT TASK

1 PLAN

Find out what sports people do in your class. Do a survey, and then create an infographic to show your results.

1 Choose the sports for your questions.
2 Write your questions about sports. Use the questions in Exercise 3, or make new questions.
3 Do the survey with your friends in class.
4 Design your infographic. Include two or three ways to show the information.
5 Check grammar, spelling, and punctuation.

2 YOUR DIGITAL PORTFOLIO

Upload your infographic to the class portfolio for everyone to see! Present your infographic to the class.

3 REFLECT

Which is your favorite infographic? Why?

CLASS 7A SURVEY ABOUT SPORTS

34 STUDENTS

There are 12 girls and 22 boys in Class 7A.

22 PLAY SOCCER

7 girls and 15 boys can play soccer.

5 girls and 7 boys can't play soccer.

16 RUN

6 girls and 10 boys can run fast.

6 girls and 12 boys can't run fast.

21 DANCE

12 girls and 9 boys can dance.

13 boys boys can't dance.

20 PLAY BASKETBALL

8 girls and 12 boys can play basketball.

4 girls and 10 boys can't play basketball.

34 SWIM

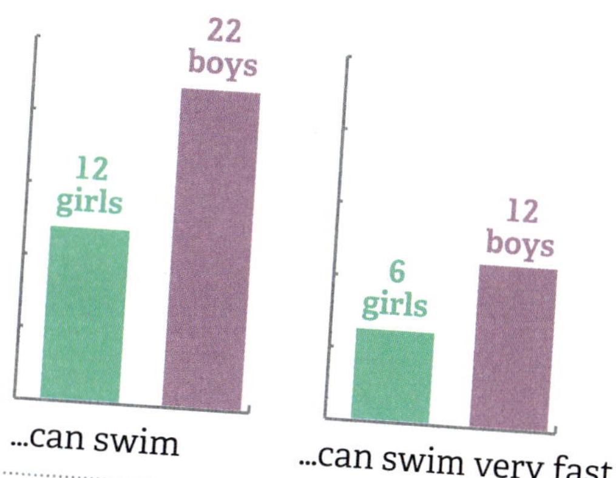

Don't forget to do exercise for **60** minutes a day! It's good for you!

VERB LIST

Verb	Unit	Page
ask	5	56
be	1	12
become	6	66
bring	7	82
buy	7	78
catch	8	87
chat	5	56
close	7	78
come	6	66
communicate	2	26
compete	8	92
cost	6	66
create	8	93
dance	8	86
develop	8	92
do	5	54
dress	7	82
drink	8	90
eat	6	72
exist	2	24
feel	8	92
finish	5	56
fly	5	61
forget	6	66
get	7	78
get up	5	54
go	5	54
go out	5	62
guess	2	22

Verb	Unit	Page
hang out	5	58
happen	6	71
hate	6	67
have	4	44
help	6	66
hope	5	56
ice-skate	8	86
improve	8	92
increase	8	92
kick	8	87
know	5	60
learn	6	69
like	5	56
listen	0	8
live	5	58
look	0	8
love	4	48
mean	0	8
meet	0	4
mind	5	60
order	6	66
play	5	54
post	2	22
practice	5	60
protect	7	82
put on	8	91
read	0	8
reduce	8	92
represent	6	71

Verb	Unit	Page
run	8	86
see	6	70
sell	6	67
send	7	82
show	7	82
sit	7	82
ski	8	86
speak	2	26
spell	0	8
spend	5	61
start	5	56
stay	6	67
study	5	56
surf	8	86
swim	8	86
take	5	54
talk	2	22
teach	6	66
text	6	66
think	6	70
throw	8	87
travel	5	60
use	2	25
walk	8	87
watch	5	56
wear	7	77
work	5	56
write	0	8

WORKBOOK CONTENTS

1 WHO Am I?

LANGUAGE REFERENCE

Verb *to be*: Affirmative, Negative, and *Wh-* Questions

Affirmative (+)		Negative (-)	
Long Form	**Short Form**	**Long Form**	**Short Form**
I **am** English.	I**'m** Spanish.	I **am not** English.	I**'m not** Brazilian.
You **are** my friend.	You**'re** my teacher.	You **are not** a student.	You**'re no**t a teacher.
He/She/It **is** my cat.	He**'s**/She**'s**/It**'s** my dog.	He/She/It **is not** my dog.	He**'s**/She**'s**/It**'s not** my cat.
We **are** students.	We**'re** friends.	We **are not** sisters.	We**'re not** sisters.
You **are** Brazilian.	You**'re** English.	You **are not** brothers.	You**'re not** brothers.
They **are** my sisters.	They**'re** my brothers.	They **are not** teachers.	They**'re not** teachers.

We use *not* in the negative form.

Simple Present (*I, you, we, they*): *Yes/No* Questions and *Wh-* Questions

Wh- Questions	Answers
How old **are** you?	I**'m** 13.
What **is** your last name?	It**'s** Adams.
What **is** your phone number?	It**'s** 555-6566.
Who **is** your doctor?	It**'s** Oliver.

We use *wh-* question word + *am/are/is* + subject in the question form.

Personal Possessions

awesome
bike
cell phone
clothes
favorite
home
jeans
music
school
school uniform
sports

Personal Information

address
age
first name
grade
last name
phone number
school's name

VOCABULARY

1 **Find six words for favorite things in the word snake.**

lifbikewvclothespoaesportsermcjeansosshomedwopemusicjir

1 bike
2 ......
3 ......
4 ......
5 ......
6 ......

2 **Match the sentences and the words.**

1 My teachers are here.
2 They are blue.
3 Soccer and swimming are examples.
4 It is small. It is in my bag.

a jeans
b cell phone
c school
d sports

3 **Put the letters in order to make words. Complete the sentences.**

1 gea age
2 rstif mane ......
3 edgar ......
4 ddrssea ......
5 oneph munreb ......
6 stal mena ......

1 My ...... is 555-0914.
2 I am in 6th ....
3 What is Martina's age? She's 12.
4 His ...... is Peter.
5 Her ...... is 134 Green Street, Oxford.
6 My ...... is Smith.

4 **Write the correct words in the chart.**

School Soccer Competition	
School	
School's Name	Weston Academy
......	514 Maple Street, Springtown
Student	
......	Angela
......	Taylor
......	11 years old
......	6th
......	555-3156

GRAMMAR

1 **Complete the sentences with *am*, *are*, or *is*.**

1 She ___is___ my mom.
2 Harry ______ my brother.
3 I ______ at home.
4 We ______ at school.
5 Toby ______ our dog.
6 You ______ my friend.
7 They ______ students.

2 **Write the sentences using short forms of the verb *to be*.**

1 He is here. ___He's here.___
2 I am not a teacher. ______
3 You are not a student. ______
4 He is 14 years old. ______
5 They are my mom and dad. ______
6 She is not my friend. ______
7 We are sisters. ______

3 **Look at the images and complete the sentences with the correct form of *to be*. Use short forms.**

1

Mrs. Eaton ___'s___ a teacher.
She ___'s not___ a doctor.

2

Toby ______ black.
He ______ white.

3

I ______ a student.
I ______ a teacher.

4

She ______ my friend.
She ______ my mom.

5

We ______ adults.
We ______ children.

4 **Complete the conversation. Use short forms.**

A Hi. [1] ___I'm___ Mrs. Jones, the new English teacher. [2] ______ your name?

B Adriana Santos.

A How old [3] ______?

B [4] ______ 13 years old.

A [5] ______ your address?

B It's 23 Elm Street.

A [6] ______ your French teacher?

B It's Mrs. Oliveira. [7] ______ my friend's mom.

READING

1 Look at the text. Check (✓) the correct answer.

1 What is it?

◯ a presentation in class ◯ an email

2 What is it for?

◯ for Paola's family ◯ to tell the class about Paola

1

2

3

4

a My parents are Marco and Rosa. They're teachers.

b My favorite food is pasta. It's a traditional food in Italy.

c I am Paola and my brother is Lorenzo. We're students.

d Bubbles is my cat. She's black and white.

2 Match the images (1-4) with the sentences (a-d).

1 ....
2 ....
3 ....
4 ....

3 Write the names.

1 Paola's brother ....
2 Paola's parents ....
3 Paola's cat ....

4 Read the presentation again and find ...

1 a job ....
2 a food ....
3 a country ....
4 an animal ....

2 ENGLISH EVERYWHERE!

LANGUAGE REFERENCE

Verb *to be*: *Yes/No* Questions and *Where ... from?*

Yes / No questions	Short answers	
Am I happy?	Yes, I **am**.	No, I**'m not**.
Are you in Tokyo?	Yes, you **are**.	No, you**'re not**.
Is he from France?	Yes, he **is**.	No, he**'s not**.
Is she from the USA?	Yes, she **is**.	No, she**'s not**.
Is it Spain?	Yes, it **is**.	No, it**'s not**.
Are we Brazilian?	Yes, we **are**.	No, we**'re not**.
Are they from Brazil?	Yes, they **are**.	No, they**'re not**.
Where ... from?		
Where am I from?	**I'm from** Spain.	**I'm not from** Spain.
Where are you from?	**You're from** France.	**You're not from** French.
Where are they from?	**They're from** Mexico.	**They're not from** Mexico.
Where's he/she/it from?	**He's/She's/It's from** South Africa.	**He's/She's/It's not from** South Africa.

Possessive ('s)

Possessive ('s)
João**'s** first language (the first language of João)
Paris**'s** restaurants (the restaurants of Paris)
The children**'s** favorite food (the favorite food of the children)
My parents**'** car (the car of my parents)

Countries and Nationalities

American
Brazil
Brazilian
British
France
French
Japan
Japanese
Mexican
Mexico
Russia
Russian
South Africa
South African
Spain
Spanish
the United Kingdom / the UK
the United States / the USA

Personal Pronouns and Possessive Adjectives

Personal Pronouns	Possessive Adjectives
I am American.	**My** language is English.
You are a good teacher.	**Your** lessons are interesting.
He is a doctor.	**His** name is Kazuo.
She is from Mexico.	**Her** nationality is Mexican.
It is a big hotel.	**Its** name is the Grand Hotel.
We are soccer fans.	**Our** favorite team is Liverpool.
They are Spanish.	**Their** country is Spain.

English Words in Many Languages

chocolate
hamburger
hotel
jeans
ketchup
pizza
restaurant
taxi

VOCABULARY

1 Circle the correct word.

1 My friend Haruki is *Japan* / *Japanese.*
2 Yves speaks *France* / *French.*
3 Helen is from London, in *the United Kingdom* / *British.*
4 Luiz is *Brazil* / *Brazilian.*
5 Johannesburg is in *South Africa* / *South African.*
6 Maria is from *Mexico* / *Mexican.*

2 Complete the sentences.

1 Pierre is from France. His language is French.
2 Juanita is from Mexico. She is ________.
3 Gabriel is Brazilian. He is from ________.
4 Scott is from New York. He is ________.
5 Diane is American. She is from ________.
6 Alla is from Russia. She speaks ________.

3 Put the letters in order and then complete the chart.

1 colchotae chocolate
2 germburha ________
3 sneaj ________
4 ixat ________
5 aursternat ________
6 tleho ________
7 zzapi ________
8 puektch ________

Food	Transportation	Clothes	Places
chocolate	t________	j________	r________
h________			h________
p________			
k________			

4 Look at the images and complete the crossword.

Down

1 

2 

3 

6 

Across

4 

5 

7 

GRAMMAR

1 Match the questions (1–6) with the short answers (a–f).

1 Are your parents teachers?
2 Is Maria from Spain?
3 Are you a soccer fan?
4 Are you and Yuko students?
5 Is Peter in his bedroom?
6 Is your house big?

a Yes, we are.
b No, he's not.
c No, she's not.
d No, it's not.
e Yes, they are.
f Yes, I am.

2 Complete the conversation. Use the correct forms of *to be*.

Olivia [1] ....Is.... Katarina your sister?
Ben No, she [2] .... She's my friend.
Olivia Oh, OK. [3] .... you and Katarina from the United Kingdom?
Ben No, we [4] .... We're American.
Olivia And [5] .... your first language English?
Ben Yes, it [6] .... But Katarina speaks French, too, because her parents are French.

3 Complete the sentences with the possessive ('s).

My Cat

1

My ....cat's.... bed.

My Friend Ying

2

My friend .... backpack.

My Brothers

3

My .... bedroom.

Boris

4

.... new bike.

My Parents

5

My .... car.

4 Find six mistakes in the text. Cross them out and write the correct words.

This is ~~a~~ friend Carlo. He lives in the United States with he family. His sister's name is Violet. Her is six years old. They parents have a restaurant in San Francisco. It name is Al Fresco. Carlo and Violet speak English and Italian because they mom is from Italy.

1 ....my....
2 ....
3 ....
4 ....
5 ....
6 ....

READING

1 Look at the class survey. What is it for? Check (✓) the correct answer.

○ to get information about the students' families
○ to get information about languages the students speak
○ to give information about countries

THE INTERNATIONAL SCHOOL | *Class Language Survey*

CLASS LANGUAGE SURVEY

Instructions: Write about where your family is from and what languages you speak. Then ask two friends.

	Your Name: *Alex*	*My mother is from the United States and my father is Mexican. At home, we speak English.*
	**Friend 1's** Name: *Sylvia*	*My mother is Spanish and my father is French. I speak Spanish to my mother and French to my father.*
	**Friend 2's** Name: *Hideki*	*My mother and father are from Japan. We speak Japanese at home.*
	**Friend 3's** Name: *Lakshmi*	*My mother is from South Africa and my father is Brazilian. We speak English at home.*

2 Check (✓) correct person.

	Alex	Sylvia	Hideki	Lakshmi
1 This person's parents are from the same country.	○	○	✓	○
2 This person's father is from France.	○	○	○	○
3 This person's parents are from Japan.	○	○	○	○
4 This person's father is from Brazil.	○	○	○	○
5 This person's mother is American.	○	○	○	○

3 Answer with one word.

1 What nationality is Alex's mother? *American*
2 Where is Sylvia's mother from? ____________
3 Where is Sylvia's father from? ____________
4 What nationality are Hideki's parents? ____________
5 Where is Lakshmi's father from? ____________

4 Write short answers to the questions.

1 Is Alex's father Russian? *No, he's not.*
2 Is English the language Alex speaks at home? ____________
3 Is Spanish the language Sylvia speaks to her mother? ____________
4 Is Hideki's mother Brazilian? ____________
5 Is Lakshmi's mother South African? ____________

3 WHERE'S HOME?

LANGUAGE REFERENCE

There is/There are

Affirmative (+)	Negative (-)
There is *a big bathroom.*	***There isn't*** a sofa in the living room.
There are *three bedrooms.*	***There aren't*** *any flowers in the yard.*

We use *there is* or *there are* to say what things are in a place.
We use *isn't* or *aren't* in the negative form.

There is/There are: Yes/No Questions

Yes/No Questions	Short Answers
Is there *a TV in your bedroom?*	*Yes,* ***there is****.* *No,* ***there isn't****.*
Are there *any chairs in the yard?*	*Yes,* ***there are****.* *No,* ***there aren't****.*

We use *is* or *are* + *there* in the question form.

Parts of a House

bathroom
bedroom
dining room
kitchen
living room
yard

Adjectives

awesome
big
modern
nice
old
small

Furniture

bed
chair
closet
door
shower
table
wall
window

VOCABULARY

1 Find six adjectives in the word search.

A	Y	I	K	D	O	L	D
B	N	N	A	S	C	M	I
C	B	I	P	U	I	O	B
Y	W	C	Q	T	Y	D	F
A	W	E	S	O	M	E	H
T	C	S	M	F	R	R	I
Z	V	F	A	E	J	N	O
U	Y	H	L	D	G	S	W
B	I	G	L	C	B	X	A

2 Put the letters in order. Then use the words to complete the sentences.

a thicken ....kitchen........
b gindni moro ....
c dary ....
d morobed ....
e thromoab ....
f nligiv mroo ....

1 There's a big refrigerator in the ....kitchen........ .
2 There are lots of flowers in the ....
3 There are two beds in the ....
4 There's a sofa in the ....
5 There is shampoo in the ....
6 There is a big table in the ....

3 Match the words below with the images.

• bed • chair • ~~closet~~ • door • shower • table • wall • window

1 
........closet........

2 
....

3 
....

4 
....

5 
....

4 Read the clues and circle the correct word.

1 There's a person in this.
(a) bed b wall c table

2 There are clothes in this.
a chair b window c closet

3 There is food on this.
a door b table c wall

4 There's a person on this.
a closet b chair c window

5 There is water in this.
a shower b bed c closet

GRAMMAR

1 What is in the image? Complete the sentences with *is*, *are*, *isn't*, and *aren't*.

1 There ....is.... a green sofa.
2 There .... a TV.
3 There .... some books.
4 There .... a dog.
5 There .... a computer.
6 There .... any people.

2 Circle the correct answers.

1 There *is* / (*are*) three cars.
2 *Are* / *Is* there a shower?
3 *Are* / *Is* there any beds?
4 There *are* / *is* a nice sofa.
5 There *aren't* / *isn't* any flowers.
6 There *aren't* / *isn't* a table.

3 Look at the image. Answer these questions with short answers.

1 Is there a blue sofa? ....No, there isn't....
2 Is there a table? ....
3 Are there any books? ....
4 Is there a closet? ....
5 Are there any black chairs? ....

4 Complete the conversation with the words below.

• are there • is there • there are (2x) • ~~there is~~ • there isn't

Sophie Do you like your new bedroom?
Marie Yes, I love it. It's very nice, and [1] ....there is.... a big blue chair in it.
Sophie [2] .... a closet?
Marie No, [3] ...., but [4] .... two big windows.
Sophie [5] .... a lot of books?
Marie Yes, [6] ....! I love books.

READING

1 **Look at the texts and check (✓) the correct answers.**

1 **What are they about?**
◯ restaurants and cafés
◯ houses and apartments

2 **What are they for?**
◯ to say if houses or apartments are good or bad
◯ to describe someone's new home

Review
★★★★

A
This is a very nice apartment! It's big and comfortable. There is a beautiful living room with a very big TV! There are two small bedrooms, and there's a nice, modern kitchen. There isn't a yard, but there is a small balcony with a lot of beautiful plants. There is only one problem – there aren't any restaurants near the apartment, and there is only one small food store.

Akira
From Tokyo, Japan. 7/15/2020

Review
★★★★★

B
This is a really nice house. It is small, but it is very warm. There is a small living room with a very comfortable sofa and a lot of books and plants – it really feels like home! There's a nice kitchen and a modern bathroom. There are a lot of good restaurants and cafés nearby. Five stars!

Gabrielle
From Paris, France. 8/12/2020

2 **Write *T* (true) or *F* (false) next to the statements.**

1 Akira says the apartment is nice and small. ....
2 Akira says there are two bedrooms in the apartment. ....
3 Akira says there is a yard with the apartment. ....
4 Gabrielle says the house is small but comfortable. ....
5 Gabrielle says there aren't any restaurants near the house. ....

3 **Answer with one word.**

1 In Akira's review, what is in the living room? ....
2 In Akira's review, which room is modern? ....
3 In Akira's review, where are the plants? ....
4 In Gabrielle's review, what is comfortable? ....
5 In Gabrielle's review, there are many plants and ....

4 FAMILY MATTERS

LANGUAGE REFERENCE

Verb *to have*: Affirmative

Affirmative (+)	
I, you, we, they	***he, she, it***
I **have** two uncles.	My friend **has** a new baby brother.
You **have** a brother.	
We **have** a lot of cousins.	She **has** two sisters.
My friends **have** parents from different countries.	My family **has** a traditional structure.

We use *have* to talk about possession.

Verb *to have* (*I, you, he, she*): Negative and *Yes/No* Questions

Negative (-)	*Yes/No* Questions	Short Answers
I **don't have** a brother You **don't have** cousins.	**Do** you **have** a brother? **Do** you **have** cousins?	Yes, I **do**. No, I **don't**.
He **doesn't have** a dad. She **doesn't have** a brother.	**Does** he **have** an uncle? **Does** she **have** a sister?	Yes, he **does**. No, she **doesn't**.

We use *don't* or *doesn't* in the negative form.
We use *do* or *does* + subject + verb in the question form.

Family Members

aunt
brother
cousin
dad
grandma
grandpa
grandparents
mom
parents
sister
uncle

Describing People

blue
brown
dark
eyes
fair
green
hair
long
short
tall

VOCABULARY

1 Put the letters in order to make words for family members.

1 therorb ......brother......
2 tnau ....
3 pargraentsnd ....
4 ertssi ....
5 apdngra ....
6 lecun ....

2 Complete the sentences.

1 My aunt Diana is my dad's ......sister.......
2 Andrew is my dad's brother. He's my ....
3 Ruby is my mom's mom. She's my ....
4 My aunt has two children. They're my ....
5 Henry is my grandpa. He's my mom's ....
6 My parents have two children. They're my .... Max and me.

3 Circle the correct word to complete the sentences.

1 My sister has *dark* / *long* eyes.
2 Julia has *tall* / *fair* hair.
3 Tom is very *tall* / *long*.
4 I have *short* / *brown* eyes.
5 Lucas has *tall* / *long* hair.
6 My grandma is very *long* / *short*.

4 Look at the image and use the words below to complete the text.

• blue • dark • eyes • hair • long • tall

This is my aunt Elisa with my uncle Jamie. Aunt Elisa has [1] ...., fair [2] .... She has [3] .... eyes. Uncle Jamie has short, [4] .... hair. His [5] .... are brown. He isn't very [6] ....

GRAMMAR

1 **Complete the conversation with *has* or *have*.**

Hannah I [1] ___have___ a very big family! My dad [2] ________ six brothers, and my mom [3] ________ three brothers and three sisters.

Ethan So you [4] ________ twelve aunts and uncles!

Hannah Yes. And my brothers and I [5] ________ 35 cousins!

Ethan Cool! I only [6] ________ one uncle and no cousins.

2 **Look at the images. Make sentences with the words in parentheses and *have* or *has.***

Claudia and Felipe / cell phones

1

Claudia and Felipe have cell phones.

Alonzo / two sisters

2

____

my aunt / a new car

3

____

Rio and Latifa / a dog

4

____

our house / a big kitchen

5

____

my grandma / two sisters

6

____

3 **Complete the conversation with *do, does, don't,* and *doesn't*.**

Antonio [1] ___Do___ you have any brothers, Fernanda?

Fernanda No, I [2] ________. I have one sister.

Antonio [3] ________ your sister have children?

Fernanda Yes, she [4] ________. He's one day old, and he [5] ________ have a name!

4 **Complete the questions and the short answers so they are true for you.**

1 ___Does___ Laura ___have___ a backpack? ___Yes___, she ___does___.

2 ________ your dad ________ a red car? ________, he ________.

3 ________ you ________ a big family? ________, I ________.

4 ________ your friend ________ black shoes? ________, she ________.

5 ________ you ________ a nice bike? ________, I ________.

6 ________ your brother ________ a cat? ________, he ________.

READING

1 Look at Rachel's and Sophia's emails. Write their names under the images.

PE Hi!
inbox

Rachel
to Sophia
at 6:20 P.M.

Hi, Sophia!
My name is Rachel. I live with my mom and my uncle in an apartment in San Francisco. My family is very small. I don't have any brothers or sisters.
My dad and my aunt live with my grandma and grandpa in a big house in the country. I go there on weekends. They have a lot of animals, for example, cats, dogs, and horses. I love it there!
Write soon!
Your new friend,
Rachel

PE classes
inbox

Sophia
to me
at 7:10 P.M.

Dear Rachel,
Thank you for your email!
My family is very different! I have two sisters and three brothers. We live with our mom and dad in a big house near Madrid. My mom is Spanish and my dad is Chinese.
I have lots of aunts and uncles, and they are married to people from different countries. We have a lot of big family parties. They are fun!
Bye for now!

Sophia

1

..................................'s family

2

..................................'s family

2 Check (✓) correct person.

	Rachel	Sophia
1 She has a big family.	○	✓
2 She doesn't have brothers and sisters.	○	○
3 She has a small family.	○	○
4 Her grandparents have a big house.	○	○
5 Her family has big parties.	○	○

5 A DAY IN THE LIFE

LANGUAGE REFERENCE

Simple Present (*I, you, we, they*): Affirmative and Negative

Affirmative (+)	Negative (-)
I **go** to school at 8:00. You **take** a shower in the morning. We **play** volleyball at school. They **have** dinner with their family.	I **don't go** to school on Sundays. You **don't take** a shower in the evening. We **don't play** football at school. They **don't have** dinner with their friends.

We use the simple present to talk about things that we often do.

We use *don't* in the negative form for *I*, *you*, *we*, and *they*.

Simple Present (*I, you, we, they*): *Yes/No* Questions and *Wh-* Questions

Yes/No Questions	Short Answers
Do you **do** your homework before dinner? **Do** they **go** to bed at 9:00?	Yes, I **do**./No, I **don't**. Yes, they **do**./No, they **don't**.
***Wh-* Questions**	**Answers**
What do you **do** after school? **What time do** they **go** to school? **Where do** they **play** soccer?	I **do** my homework and have dinner. They **go** to school at 7:30. They **play** soccer in the park.

We use *do* + subject + verb in the question form.

Daily Routines

do my homework
get up
go home
go to bed
go to school
have breakfast
have dinner
play volleyball
take a shower
take the bus

Free-time Activities

go to restaurants
hang out with friends
listen to music
play soccer
play video games
watch movies

VOCABULARY

1 Complete each sentence with a word.

• do • ~~get up~~ • go • have • play • take (2x)

1 I ___get up___ at 10:00 on the weekend.

2 Sue and Ben ______ volleyball after school.

3 I ______ breakfast with my mom and sister.

4 We ______ our homework in the evening.

5 ______ a shower every morning.

6 We ______ the bus to school.

7 They ______ home at 3:30.

2 Match the beginnings (1–5) with the endings (a-e).

1 My sister and I have — d

2 Beth and I go to

3 Rosie and Grace play

4 After dinner, I do

5 On the weekend, I get

a my homework.

b up at 10 a.m.

c school at 8 a.m.

d dinner at 6 p.m.

e volleyball on the weekend.

3 Complete the text using the letters to help you.

What do I do on the weekend? Well, on Saturdays, I [1] ___hang out___ (angh tou) with my friends. We [2] ______ (tensil ot) music in my bedroom and we also [3] ______ (lapy) video games. Sometimes we [4] ______ (thawc) movies. On Sundays, I [5] ______ (yapl) soccer in the park with my brother. Then we [6] ______ (og ot) a restaurant with our parents. I love weekends!

4 Match the phrases with the images.

• go to restaurants • ~~hang out with friends~~ • listen to music
• play soccer • play video games • watch movies

1

___hang out with friends___

2

______

3

______

4

______

5

______

6

______

GRAMMAR

1 Complete the sentences about each image, one affirmative and one negative.

1

We ___play___ tennis. (play)

We ___don't play___ soccer. (play)

2

I ______ to school with my friend Rachel. (go)

I ______ to school with my brother. (go)

3
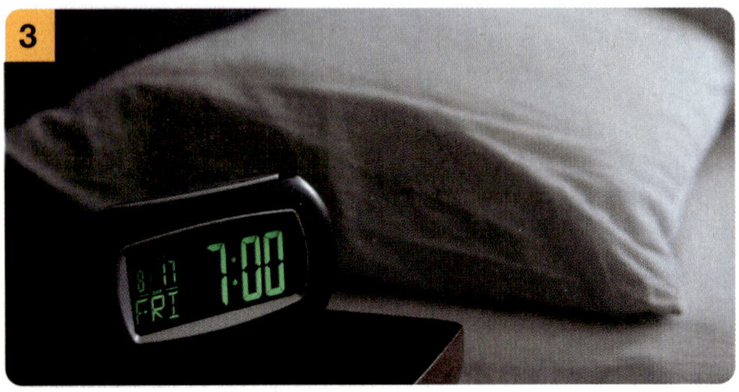

They ______ at seven o'clock. (get up)

They ______ at eight o'clock. (get up)

4

I ______ breakfast with my brother. (have)

I ______ breakfast with my parents. (have)

2 Circle the correct words in the *Wh-* questions.

1 *Where* / (*What*) do you do on Saturday afternoon?

2 *Where* / *What* do they go swimming?

3 *Where* / *What* time do you come home?

4 *Where* / *What* do they eat for dinner?

3 Complete the short dialogues with the words below.

• do (2x) • ~~what~~ • where

1 **Tom** ___What___ do you do on Sundays?

Amy I hang out with my friends.

2 **Daniel** ______ they play video games?

Lara Yes, they do.

3 **Sophia** Do you do your homework on the weekend?

Isabel Yes, I ______.

4 **Abbie** ______ do they listen to music?

Oscar They listen to music in their bedroom.

4 Match the questions (1–4) and the answers (a–d).

1 Do you go to school on a bus? — c

2 What time do you go to bed?

3 Where do you have dinner?

4 Do you play sports?

a Yes, I play volleyball and soccer.

b At home with my family.

c No, I don't. I walk there.

d At ten o'clock.

READING

Hey, Mom. Can you chat now? 11:20 a.m.

Sure! Nice to hear from you, Rachel! How are you? 11:20 a.m.

Good, thanks. Everything is fine here. I love this city – it's beautiful. I'm so happy to be here at this summer camp. 11:20 a.m.

Great! Tell me about your day. What do you do? 11:22 a.m.

Well, I get up early during the week, at 7:00, and I have breakfast in my room here. Then, I read a little and then I take the bus to school. I study all day and then I go home at 6:00. 11:23 a.m.

That sounds good. What about lunch? Do you have lunch? 11:23 a.m.

Yes, I do! Don't worry! 🙂 I have a sandwich with my friends. 11:24 a.m.

Nice! And what about the evenings? What do you do? Do you hang out with your new friends? 11:25 a.m.

Yeah! There are some really nice people here. I have four or five new friends. 11:25 a.m.

That's great! Do you eat together in the evenings? 11:25 a.m.

Yes, we do. It's fun! Talk soon, Mom! ❤❤❤ 11:27 a.m.

Bye, my love. 😚 11:27 a.m.

1 Look at the text and answer the questions.

1 What is it?

◯ an email ◯ messages on social media

2 What is the purpose of the text?

◯ to say something important ◯ to say hello and chat

2 Circle the correct answer for Rachel.

1 I get up early *on the weekend* / *during the week*.

2 After breakfast, I *read* / *watch TV*.

3 I *take the bus* / *walk* to school.

4 In the evening, I *study* / *hang out* with friends.

5 In the evening, I have dinner *with other people* / *alone*.

3 Answer the questions.

1 What time do you get up? I get up at 7:00.

2 Where do you have breakfast? ______

3 What do you do all day? ______

4 What do you have for lunch? ______

6 SCHOOL TIME

LANGUAGE REFERENCE

Simple Present (*he*, *she*, *it*): Affirmative and Negative

Affirmative (+)	Negative (-)
Peter **plays** volleyball.	Adam **doesn't play** soccer.
Polly **chats** with her friends.	He **doesn't chat** with his friends.
Ollie **watches** TV.	She **doesn't watch** TV on Mondays.
The class **starts** at 10:00.	It **doesn't start** at 10:00 on Fridays.

We add *-s* or *-es* to the verbs after *he*, *she* and *it*.
We use *doesn't* in the negative form.

Simple Present (*he*, *she*, *it*): *Yes/No* Questions, *Wh-* Questions

Yes/No Questions	Short Answers
Does he **like** math?	Yes, he **does**./No, he **doesn't**.
Does she **have** a pet?	Yes, she **does**./No, she **doesn't**.
Does it **start** at 4:00?	Yes, it **does**./No, it **doesn't**.
***Yes/No* Questions**	**Short Answers**
Where does he **work**?	He **works** in a school.
When does she **do** her homework?	She **does** her homework in the evening.
How often **does** the restaurant **close**?	It **closes** once a year.

We use *does* + subject + verb in the question form.

Verbs

don't like
hate
like
love

School Subjects

art
computer science
English
geography
history
math
music
physical education (PE)
science
Spanish

Places in a School

athletic field
cafeteria
gymnasium
library
maker lab
principal's office
restrooms
science lab
teachers' lounge

VOCABULARY

1 Find nine school subjects in the word search.

S	T	M	A	T	H	I	N	G	S
C	L	U	I	R	L	G	U	G	C
I	E	S	P	U	O	R	M	E	I
E	C	I	Q	M	W	A	L	O	L
N	E	C	U	F	E	R	A	G	P
C	R	O	H	I	S	T	O	R	Y
E	T	O	O	G	X	A	D	A	V
C	S	P	A	N	I	S	H	P	Z
R	F	E	L	K	I	C	B	H	S
E	N	G	L	I	S	H	Y	Y	D

2 Complete sentences for you with *like* (☺), *don't like* (☹), *love* (☺ ☺), or *hate* (☹☹) and the subject in the picture.

1 

2 

3 

4 

3 Match the images with the words below.

- athletic field
- cafeteria
- gymnasium
- library
- maker lab
- principal's office
- restrooms
- teachers' lounge

1 
athletic field

2 

3 

4 

5 

6 

7 

8 

4 Use words from the images to complete the sentences.

1 We make things in the maker lab.
2 We read books in the ....
3 We wash our hands in the ....
4 We play basketball in the ....
5 Mrs. Smith goes to the .... at lunchtime.

GRAMMAR

1 Correct the mistake in these sentences.

1 Grace don't hang out with her friends.
Grace doesn't hang out with her friends.

2 Martin watchs TV after school.
....

3 Roberto doesn't plays the piano.
....

4 History class start at 10:00.
....

5 Mariona don't do her homework in her bedroom.
....

2 Look at the images. Then use the verb in parentheses to complete the sentences.

1

Clara doesn't get up at six o'clock. (get up)

2

Dan .... in the living room. (study)

3

Mr. Ellis .... PE. (teach)

4

Salim .... pizza. (like)

5

Alice .... to school with her friends. (go)

6

Fatima .... soccer. (coach)

3 Put the words in order to make a conversation.

brother / like / video games / Does / your / ?
Ed ....

doesn't / No, / he
Liam ....

he / in the / do / What / evening / does
Ed ....

studies / in / He / bedroom / his
Liam ....

have / he / Does / friends
Ed ....

he / Yes, / does. / soccer / He / with them / plays / on Saturdays
Liam ....
....

4 Complete the *Wh-* questions to match the answers.

1 Where does Sam play soccer?
He plays soccer in the park.

2 .... you .... volleyball? I play volleyball every day.

3 .... Nadia .... for lunch? She has a sandwich for lunch.

4 .... Max .... volleyball? He plays volleyball on Friday.

5 .... your sister .... to college? She goes to college in New York.

6 .... your science class .... ? It starts at 11:00.

READING

1 Look at the text. What is it? Check (✓) the correct option.

- ○ an advertisement for a sports club
- ○ a magazine article about adolescents
- ○ information about a school

MEET SOME OF OUR STUDENTS!

SANDRA

Sandra loves sports. She goes to the gymnasium after school. She has PE on Mondays and Thursdays, and she is on the school volleyball team. On weekends, she hangs out with her friends and listens to music. ■

FUNSANI

Funsani plays the guitar and sings in a band. His favorite thing is movies. He goes to the school's Movie Club every Wednesday, and he always goes to the movies with his friends on weekends. ■

GEMMA

Gemma studies a lot. She likes English and math, but her favorite subject is history. She is a member of our school History Club. She doesn't like sports, but she loves music and she plays the piano. ■

ANTON

Anton is one of our school's best artists. He makes big paintings. He also likes drama, and he goes to the Theater Club on Saturdays. Anton's favorite thing is video games. He plays online with friends from all over the world. ■

2 Read the text and check (✓) the correct person.

	Sandra	Funsani	Gemma	Anton
1 good at art	○	○	○	✓
2 listens to music	○	○	○	○
3 loves movies	○	○	○	○
4 has friends all over the world	○	○	○	○
5 doesn't like sports	○	○	○	○
6 sings in a band	○	○	○	○

3 Read the text again and answer the questions.

1 Where does Sandra go after school?

She goes to the gymnasium.

2 What team is Sandra on?

....

3 Who goes to the movies with Funsani?

....

4 What instrument does Funsani play?

....

5 What instrument does Gemma play?

....

6 What club does Anton go to?

....

7 WHAT'S HE WEARING?

LANGUAGE REFERENCE

Present Progressive: Affirmative and Negative

Affirmative (+)	Negative (-)
I'**m wearing** a red T-shirt.	I'**m not wearing** a blue T-shirt.
You'**re wearing** a dress.	You'**re not wearing** a skirt.
He'**s having** dinner.	He'**s not playing** a video game.
She'**s going** to bed.	She'**s not watching** a movie.
We'**re buying** jeans.	We'**re not buying** sneakers.
They'**re playing** soccer.	They'**re not playing** volleyball.

We use the present progressive to talk about activities that we are doing now.
We use *not* after *am*, *are,* and *is* in the negative form.

Present Progressive: *Yes/No* Questions and *Wh-* Questions

Yes/No Questions	Short Answers
Are you **doing** your homework?	Yes, I **am**. / No, I'**m not**.
Is he **wearing** a coat?	Yes, he **is**. / No, he'**s not**.
Is she **taking** a shower?	Yes, she **is**. / No, she'**s not**.
Are we **wearing** the right clothes?	Yes, we **are**. / No, we'**re not**.
Are they **having** dinner?	Yes, they **are**. / No, they'**re not**.
***Wh-* Questions**	**Answers**
What **are** you **doing**?	I'**m having** breakfast.
Where **is** she **having** dinner?	She'**s having** dinner at Sara's house.
Who **is taking** a shower?	Dad'**s taking** a shower.

We use *are* or *is* + subject + verb in the question form.

Clothes

boots
coat
dress
glasses
hat
jacket
jeans
pants
shirt
shoes
shorts
skirt
sneakers
socks
sweatshirt
top
T-shirt
wear

VOCABULARY

1 Match the images with the words.

A 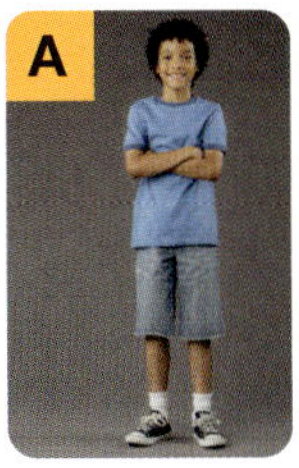

shorts, a T-shirt, and sneakers

B 

C 

D 

E 

1 a jacket and pants
2 a skirt and boots
3 glasses and a hat
4 a coat and a hat
5 ~~shorts, a T-shirt, and sneakers~~

2 Complete the sentences. Put the letters in parentheses in order to help you.

1 I don't wear pants in the summer. I wear shorts (srosht).
2 Lucas wears pants and a ______ (riths) to school.
3 My mom wears jeans and a ______ (sewatishrt) at home.
4 At school I wear shoes, but at home I wear ______ (seankres)
5 My sister wears a ______ (tsrik) and a top to the gym.

3 Find six words for clothes and accessories in the word snake.

mreosocksoptiglassestrybodresszamuvcoatsytihatuityskirtklry

1 socks
2 ______
3 ______
4 ______
5 ______
6 ______

4 Look at the images and complete the crossword.

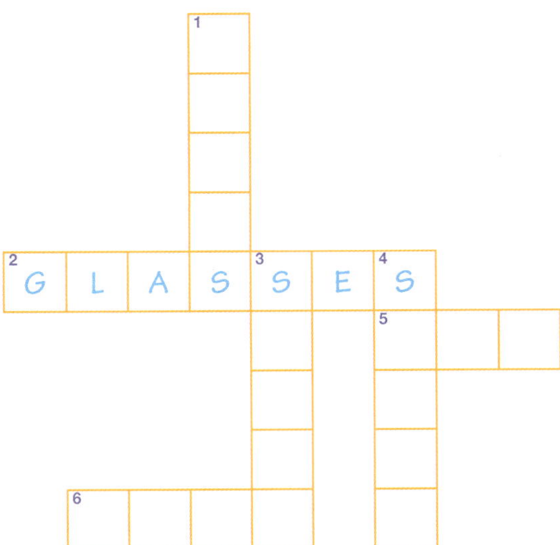

Across

2 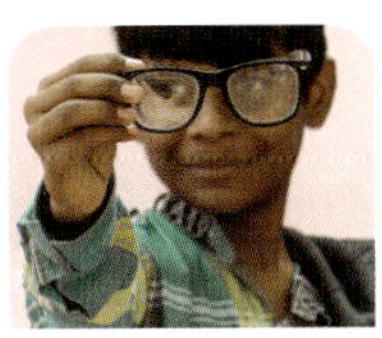

5 

6 

Down

1 

3 

4 

GRAMMAR

1 Circle the correct answer.

1 He's *wearing* / *wear* a hat.
2 They *'s* / *'re* playing soccer.
3 I'm *watch* / *watching* TV at the moment.
4 *She* / *She's* taking a shower right now.
5 We're *have* / *having* dinner.

2 Look at the images. Use the verbs to complete the present progressive sentences.

1

He 's not wearing a jacket. (wear)

2

They ______ video games. (play)

3

I ______ a coat. (wear)

4

We ______ breakfast. (have)

5

Isabel ______ her homework. (do)

3 Use the sentence clues to make questions and answers using the present progressive.

1 What / Dad / do?
have / breakfast

What is Dad doing?

He's having breakfast.

2 What / Sophia / do?
watch / movie

______

______

3 Where / Rosa / play soccer?
play soccer / park

______

______

4 What / you / wear?
wear / red dress

______

______

5 What / Lara and Jacob / do?
listen / music

______

______

4 Complete the conversation.

Mom [1] Are you having breakfast, Megan?

Megan No, [2] ______ hanging out with Joe in the living room.

Mom [3] ______ are you and Joe doing? [4] ______ you watching a movie?

Megan No, we [5] ______. We [6] ______ playing video games.

Mom What about Dad? [7] ______ he having breakfast?

Megan No, he [8] ______. He [9] ______ taking a shower at the moment.

READING

1 Read the texts and answer these questions. Circle the correct answers.

1 **Where do you see texts like this?**
a in a book
b in a magazine
c in a newspaper

2 **What are the boys describing?**
a where they are
b what they are doing
c what they are wearing

BOYS IN DIFFERENT COUNTRIES TELL US WHAT THEY ARE WEARING.

1 Luis 2 .... 3 .... 4 ....

DANIEL: So today, I'm wearing my favorite clothes because I'm hanging out with my friends, Bruno and Felipe. As you can see, I'm wearing a gray and blue shirt and some jeans. The jeans are old, but they're OK. Right now, I'm listening to some music, and I'm very happy.

GABRIEL: As you can see, I'm wearing a hat today. I like hats – I have eight or nine in different colors. This green hat is my favorite. I'm wearing a coat because it's really cold, and I'm also wearing blue pants and boots. I like my boots.

LUIS: I'm wearing my brother's pink T-shirt and my favorite green shorts. I'm also wearing my new, blue sneakers. I love sneakers. I wear them every day, but I hate boots.

LUCAS: Today I'm wearing blue shorts, an old, white T-shirt, and a hat. I'm not wearing a coat or a jacket because it's summer and it's very warm. Oh, and I'm wearing sneakers because I'm playing in the park.

2 Read the texts again and write the boys' names under the correct images.

3 Choose the correct person.

	Daniel	Gabriel	Luis	Lucas
1 ... is wearing his favorite shorts?	○	○	✓	○
2 ... is listening to music?	○	○	○	○
3 ... doesn't like boots?	○	○	○	○
4 ... has lots of hats?	○	○	○	○
5 ... is wearing a white T-shirt?	○	○	○	○

4 Are the sentences *T* (true) or *F* (false)?

1 Two boys are wearing shorts. (T) / F
2 Luis is wearing his brother's shorts. T / F
3 Three boys are wearing hats. T / F
4 Gabriel is playing in the park. T / F
5 Luis's sneakers are old and blue. T / F

8 GET MOVING!

LANGUAGE REFERENCE

Can: Ability

Affirmative (+)	Negative (-)
I **can play** soccer. He/She/It **can run** five kilometers. We **can make** pizza. You **can speak** French. They **can dance**.	I **can't play** baseball. He/She/It **can't run** five kilometers. We **can't make** pizza. You **can't speak** French. They **can't dance**.
***Yes/No* Questions**	**Short Answers**
Can I **walk**? **Can** you **play** basketball? **Can** he/she/it **catch** the ball? **Can** they **swim**?	Yes, I **can**./No, I **can't**. Yes, you **can**./No, you **can't**. Yes, he/she/it **can**. / No, he/she/it **can't**. Yes, they **can**./No, they **can't**.

We use *can* to talk about ability.

Imperatives

Affirmative (+)	Negative (-)
Kick the ball to me. **Open** your book to page 34. **Go** to room 12.	**Don't forget** your backpack. **Don't run** in the classroom. **Don't take** a bus.

We use imperatives to tell people what to do.

Verbs and Sports

catch
dance
ice-skate
kick
play volleyball
run
ski
surf
swim
throw
walk

Healthy Habits

do exercise
don't drink soda
don't eat junk food
don't go to bed late
don't sit down all day
drink water
eat healthy food
go to bed early

VOCABULARY

1 Circle the correct verb in each sentence.

1 My little sister can't *play* / *catch* / *surf* a ball.
2 Do you want to *swim* / *walk* / *kick* in the ocean?
3 Sometimes we play music and *run* / *dance* / *throw*.
4 In the winter, you can *swim* / *ski* / *ice-skate* on the lake.
5 Can you *throw* / *catch* / *run* ten kilometers?
6 We *kick* / *play* / *run* soccer in the park.

2 Complete with these verbs. Then write them in the correct column.

• do • ~~drink~~ • drink • eat • eat • go • sit down • go

1 ___drink___ soda
2 ________ to bed late
3 ________ all day
4 ________ to bed early
5 ________ healthy food
6 ________ exercise
7 ________ water
8 ________ junk food

Healthy	Unhealthy

3 Look at the images and complete the sentences with the vocabulary from Exercise 3.

1

Laura doesn't ___drink___ soda. She ___drinks water___.

2

My dad ________ at work.

3

Pablo doesn't ________ food. He ________.

4

Adela ________ at the gymnasium.

5

My little sister ________ bed early. She doesn't ________.

GRAMMAR

1 Find the mistakes. Cross out the words that are wrong and write the correct words on the lines.

Amelia Can your brother ~~plays~~ basketball, Martin?
Martin No, he don't. But he can play soccer.
Amelia I love soccer! I can to run very fast. Can't you run fast, too?
Martin No, I don't. I am very slow.
Amelia Can you throw a ball?
Martin Yes, I can. And I can catching a ball, too.
Amelia Cool!

1 play
2 ....
3 ....
4 ....
5 ....
6 ....

2 Complete the sentences with *can* or *can't* and a verb below.

• ~~catch~~ • do • make • play • run • speak

1 My sister can't catch a ball. (-)
2 .... you .... ten kilometers?
3 All my friends .... basketball. (+)
4 .... your mom .... Japanese?
5 Maria .... her math homework. (-)
6 I .... great cakes. (+)

3 Put the words in order to make imperative sentences.

1 outdoors / every / Play / day
Play outdoors every day.
2 a lot of / Don't / candy / eat
....
3 at the / fun / Have / park
....
4 the ball / Julia / Throw / to
....
5 your / brother / kick / Don't
....
6 to / book / Give / the / me
....

4 Look at the images and use the verbs below to complete affirmative and negative imperative sentences.

• catch • eat • forget • ~~go~~ • swim • walk

1
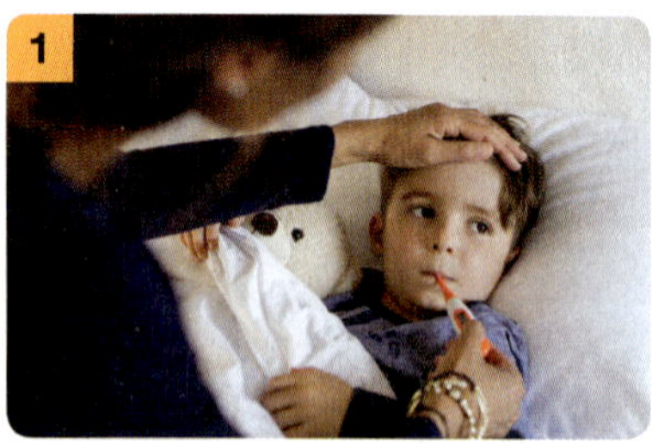
Don't go to school today!

2

.... the ball, Marco!

3

.... in the ocean today!

4

.... your vegetables, Pablo!

5

Today's hot. .... to drink water!

6

.... to school today. Take a bus!

READING

1 **Look at the posters. What are they for? Check (✓) the correct answer.**

◯ to help students be healthy
◯ to give information about school clubs
◯ to give information about sports clubs

Can't cook? We can teach you!

Try our friendly cooking club.
Come to the cooking room from 4:00 to 5:30 on Mondays. Learn to cook healthy food that tastes great, too! Don't forget, you can eat all the tasty things you make!

CAN YOU THROW AND CATCH A BALL?

Are you between the ages of 13 and 15? Come and join our basketball club!

We meet at 5:00 on Wednesdays at the gymnasium.

Join us (and our fantastic coaches, Mr. Allen and Ms. Williams!) for an hour of fun and exercise!

History isn't boring! It's great!

Do you love history, too? Join us in the school cafeteria on Fridays at lunchtime to eat lunch and talk about interesting history topics. Next week's history club topic: US presidents from 1900 to 2000. All students are welcome!

LOVE SOCCER AND HATE BAD WEATHER?

No problem! Play indoor soccer with us! We have friendly games in the school gym: girls on Tuesdays and boys on Fridays. Wear sneakers and comfortable clothes.

All ages play together.

2 **Read the posters. Are the statements *T* (true) or *F* (false)?**

1 Twelve-year-olds can join the basketball club. T /(F)
2 The cooking club is one and a half hours long. T / F
3 The soccer club is at school. T / F
4 Girls and boys play together in the soccer club. T / F
5 The history club meets in a classroom. T / F
6 The history club is at lunchtime. T / F

3 **Choose the correct ending for each sentence.**

1 Basketball club finishes at ...
 a 5:00.
 (b) 6:00.
2 Students play basketball ...
 a indoors.
 b outside.
3 Students learn to make food like ...
 a cakes, pizza, and burgers.
 b salad and vegetables.
4 Soccer club on Fridays is for ...
 a girls.
 b boys.
5 History club members eat their lunch ...
 a at the club meetings.
 b before the meetings.
6 The history club is for ...
 a all ages.
 b students aged 11–13.

Thanks and Acknowledgements

We would like to thank the following people for their invaluable contribution to the series: Cara Norris, Justine Gesell, Kate Woodford, Liz Walter, Maria Toth, Melanie Starren, S. Bastian Harris, Sue Andre Costello, and Tom Hadland.

The authors and editors would like to thank all the teachers who have contributed to the development of the course:

Geysla Lopes de Alencar, Priscila Araújo, David Williams Mocock de Araújo, Leticia da Silva Azevedo, Francisco Evangelista Ferreira Batista, Luiz Fernando Carmo, Thiago Silva Campos, Cintia Castilho, Mônica Egydio, Érica Fernandes, Viviane Azevêdo de Freitas, Marco Giovanni, Rodolfo de Aro da Rocha Keizer, Vanessa Leroy, Bruno Fernandes de Lima, Allana Tavares Maciel, Jonadab Mansur, Rogério dos Santos Melo, Carlos Ubiratã Gois de Menezes, Aryanne Moreira, Joelba Geane da Silva, Vanessa Silva Pereira, Daniela Costa Pinheiro, Isa de França Vasconcelos, Eliana Perrucci Vergani, Geraldo Vieira, Whebston Mozart.

The authors and publishers acknowledge the following sources of copyright material and are grateful for the permissions granted. While every effort has been made, it has not always been possible to identify the sources of all the material used, or to trace all copyright holders. If any omissions are brought to our notice, we will be happy to include the appropriate acknowledgements on reprinting and in the next update to the digital edition, as applicable.

Key: R = Review, U = Unit, W = Welcome

Student's Book

Photography

All the photos are sourced from Getty Images.

UW: Hispanolistic/E+; Medesulda/DigitalVision Vectors; zak00/DigitalVision Vectors; Noedelhap/iStock/Getty Images Plus; Science Photo Library; human/iStock/Getty Images Plus; Hiob/E+; **U1:** Jose Luis Pelaez Inc/DigitalVision; Suriyo Hmun Kaew/EyeEm; Soud Aldayoli/EyeEm; Mint Images/Mint Images RF; fstop123/iStock/Getty Images Plus; levente bodo/Moment; David Madison/Photographer's Choice/Getty Images Plus; Iaroslava Zolotko/EyeEm; SolStock/E+; bgblue/DigitalVision Vectors; The Good Brigade/DigitalVision; Alexthq/iStock/Getty Images Plus; Sven Hagolani; Andersen Ross Photography Inc; AndreyPopov/iStock/Getty Images Plus; AlenaMozhjer/iStock/Getty Images Plus; Slavica/E+; kali9/E+; ET-ARTWORKS/DigitalVision Vectors; fstop123/E+; Leontura/E+; JNS/Gamma-Rapho; Nick Ridley/Oxford Scientific; samxmeg/E+; sMedioimages/Photodisc; Victor_Brave/iStock/Getty Images Plus; pondsaksit/iStock/Getty Images Plus; calvindexter/DigitalVision Vectors; Kryssia Campos/Moment; Jodi Jacobson/E+; Kypros/Moment; Eric LAFFORGUE/Gamma-Rapho; Photo 12/Universal Images Group; Mike Harrington/Stone; **U2:** Mireya Acierto/Photodisc; tunejadez/iStock/Getty Images Plus; Claire Plumridge/Moment; vanillamilk/iStock/Getty Images Plus; Eric Overton/iStock/Getty Images Plus; Vectorios2016/DigitalVision Vectors; Jamie Grill/The Image Bank; Juan Silva/Stockbyte; Ronnie Kaufman/DigitalVision; Jack Hollingsworth/Photodisc; Layland Masuda/Moment Open; David Sacks/Photodisc; John D. Buffington/DigitalVision; hartcreations/E+; Jamie Grill; liangpv/DigitalVision Vectors; cveiv/iStock/Getty Images Plus; ELIKA-/iStock/Getty Images Plus; Viktorcvetkovic/iStock/Getty Images Plus; VanReeel/iStock/Getty Images Plus; Kypros/Moment; PeopleImages/E+; GelatoPlus/DigitalVision Vectors; quisp65/DigitalVision Vectors; Jeffrey Coolidge/DigitalVision; Bhimsasidhorn Osti/Moment; Jacobs Stock Photography Ltd/DigitalVision; espiegle/E+; DR NEIL OVERY/Science Photo Library; LRCImagery/iStock/Getty Images Plus; carlosrojas20/iStock/Getty Images Plus; Lepretre Pierre/Moment; Flavio Coelho/Moment; Jan-Otto/iStock Unreleased; De Agostini/W. Buss/De Agostini Picture Library; DoctorEgg/Moment; Antonio Ferreira Silva/EyeEm; IakovKalinin/iStock/Getty Images Plus; alenkadr/iStock/Getty Images Plus; Ziva_K/E+; Lew Robertson/Stone;
eli_asenova/E+; GCShutter/E+; bluecinema/iStock/Getty Images Plus; FotografiaBasica/E+; Vladone/iStock/Getty Images Plus; Mr_Khan/iStock/Getty Images Plus; kyoshino/iStock/Getty Images Plus; steve-goacher/iStock/Getty Images Plus; Tetra Images; Cimmerian/E+; polygraphus/iStock/Getty Images Plus; simoncarter/E+; chuckchee/iStock/Getty Images Plus; Illerlok_Xolms/iStock/Getty Images Plus; Turgay Malikli/iStock/Getty Images Plus; YURII ZASIMOV/iStock/Getty Images Plus; Jagoda Matejczuk/500px/500Px Plus; **R1-2:** Maksym Kapliuk/istock/Getty Images Plus; ELIKA/iStock/Getty Images Plus; VanReeel/iStock/Getty Images Plus; skynesher/E+; izusek/iStock/Getty Images Plus; numbeos/E+; Tetra Images; Westend61; **U3:** byakkaya/E+; monkeybusinessimages/iStock/Getty Images Plus; Maria Rueger/Moment; piovesempre/iStock/Getty Images Plus; John Keeble/Moment; Cyndi Monaghan/Moment; Driendl Group/Stockbyte; kpalimski/iStock/Getty Images Plus; JoKMedia/E+; cmspic/iStock/Getty Images Plus; Pipat Wongsawang/EyeEm; Bombaert Patrick/EyeEm; JazzIRT/E+; Firmafotografen/iStock/Getty Images Plus; OlegAlbinsky/E+; Busà Photography/Moment; tulcarion/E+; Martin Deja/Moment; svetikd/E+; Gerhard Zwerger-Schoner; Ilyabolotov/iStock/Getty Images Plus; _LeS_/iStock/Getty Images Plus; Peter Dazeley/The Image Bank; Lenora Gim/The Image Bank/Getty Images Plus; Pakorn Kumruen/EyeEm; Sinan Kocaslan/E+; Richard Newstead/Moment; Дмитрий Ларичев/iStock/Getty Images Plus; scibak/E+; stevenallan/iStock/Getty Images Plus; Roy JAMES Shakespeare/Photodisc; Enrique Díaz/7cero/Moment; Valerio Rosati/EyeEm; Click&Boo/Moment; Jobalou/DigitalVision Vectors; fStop Images; **U4:** Yevgen Timashov/Cultura; Amos Morgan/Photodisc; Oliver Rossi/Stone; brusinski/iStock/Getty Images Plus; quavondo/E+; Morsa Images/DigitalVision; Rubberball/Scott Hancock; stevezmina1/DigitalVision Vectors; bubaone/DigitalVision Vectors; Oliver Rossi/Stone; druvo/iStock/Getty Images Plus; Elizabeth W. Kearley/Moment Open; ET-ARTWORKS/DigitalVision Vectors; SolStock/E+; Image Source; fstop123/E+; MicrovOne/iStock/Getty Images Plus; Hill Street Studios/DigitalVision; LWA/Dann Tardif/DigitalVision; Maskot; Peathegee Inc; Ron Levine/DigitalVision; Nick David/Stone; Portra Images/Stone; Juanmonino/E+; Jose Luis Pelaez Inc/DigitalVision; LokFung/DigitalVision Vectors; E.Hanazaki Photography/Moment; Alexandre Morin-Laprise/Moment; FG Trade/E+; Marco Cristofori/Corbis; Robin Skjoldborg/DigitalVision; Sherry Galey/Moment; DocumentarySanneBerg/iStock/Getty Images Plus; **R3-4:** artisticco/iStock/Getty Images Plus; jaroon/E+; jmsilva/E+; master1305/iStock/Getty Images Plus; Jose Luis Pelaez Inc/DigitalVision; Sam Diephuis; Morsa Images/DigitalVision; Tara Moore/Stone; Cecilie_Arcurs/E+; billnoll/E+; sarahwolfephotography/Moment; FG Trade/E+; Westend61; Seth Goldfarb/Stone; Nathan Blaney/Photodisc; doodlemachine/DigitalVision Vectors; belchonock/iStock/Getty Images Plus; **U5:** Bartosz Hadyniak/E+; martinedoucet/E+; Vesna Jovanovic/EyeEm; shaunl/iStock Unreleased; vgajic/E+; Carol Yepes/Moment; southerlycourse/E+; Tetra Images - Jamie Grill/Brand X Pictures; www.flickr.com/photos/jeijiang/Moment; Sudowoodo/iStock/Getty Images Plus; Kevin Phillips/Photodisc; Calvin Chan Wai Meng/Moment; John Seaton Callahan/Moment; Caiaimage; exdez/DigitalVision Vectors; Noel Hendrickson/DigitalVision; Alexandros Maragos/Moment Open; PhotoAlto/Odilon Dimier/PhotoAlto Agency RF Collections; Hero Images; Stavros Markopoulos/Moment; MediaNews Group/The Riverside Press-Enterprise via Getty Images; Johner RF; Shestock; Enis Aksoy/DigitalVision Vectors; sesame/DigitalVision Vectors; LUNAMARINA/iStock/Getty Images Plus; Caiaimage; tunart/E+; Collin Key/Moment; Norbert Breuer/EyeEm; **U6:** Jonas Gratzer/LightRocket; greyj/iStock/Getty Images Plus; Thomas Tolstrup/DigitalVision; Ljupco/iStock/Getty Images Plus; RichLegg/iStock/Getty Images Plus; Fancy/Veer/Corbis/Getty Images Plus; Ben Welsh/The Image Bank; Mongkolchon Akesin/EyeEm; kycstudio/DigitalVision Vectors; Delpixart/iStock/Getty Images Plus; mixetto/E+; BSIP/Universal Images Group; creatingmore/E+; matsabe/iStock/Getty Images Plus; Alex Potemkin/E+; Martin Holverda/iStock/Getty Images Plus; Science Photo Library - NASA/Brand X Pictures; JOHANNES EISELE/AFP; masterSergeant/iStock/Getty Images Plus; Bruce Leighty/Photolibrary; W. Cody/Corbis; EmirMemedovski/E+; Witthaya Prasongsin/Moment; JayKay57/E+; Vitalij Cerepok/EyeEm; Nitat Termmee/Moment; Emma Kim/Cultura; Nataliia Melnyk/EyeEm; alacatr/iStock/Getty Images Plus; Ana Paola Santillan Alcocer/EyeEm; Michał Chodyra/iStock/Getty Images Plus; dottedhippo/iStock/Getty Images Plus; **R5-6:** Victor Coscaron/EyeEm; adventtr/iStock/Getty Images Plus; Raul_Wong/Moment; Shannon Fagan/The Image Bank; Wavebreakmedia/iStock/Getty Images Plus; Volodymyr Kryshtal/iStock/Getty Images Plus; **U7:** mixetto/E+; clu/E+; Suradech14/iStock/Getty Images Plus; gemenacom/iStock/Getty Images Plus; istanbulimage/E+; NAKphotos/iStock/Getty Images Plus; carlosalvarez/E+; Tat'yana Andreyeva/iStock/Getty Images Plus; studiocasper/iStock/Getty Images Plus; heinteh/iStock/Getty Images Plus; kbeis/DigitalVision Vectors; selimaksan/E+; SensorSpot/E+; Turqay Melikli/iStock/Getty Images Plus; calvindexter/DigitalVision Vectors; kolotuschenko/iStock/Getty Images Plus; Igor Petrovic/iStock/Getty Images Plus; Rakdee/DigitalVision Vectors; James Leynse/Corbis Historical; hadynyah/E+; Blaine Harrington III/The Image Bank Unreleased; duncan1890/DigitalVision Vectors; Alyson Aliano/Photodisc;
U8: hadynyah/E+; SerrNovik/iStock/Getty Images Plus; coscaron/iStock/Getty Images Plus; Westend61; Slavica/E+; Mordolff/E+; luckyvector/iStock/Getty Images Plus; 3xy/iStock/Getty Images Plus; urbancow/E+; Ascent Xmedia/Stone; Jose Luis Pelaez/Stone; Boris Streubel/Bongarts; caracterdesign/iStock/Getty Images Plus; Lionel Bonaventure/AFP;